"A worthy and comprehensive primer for anyon[   ]
how to pull off—raising sons to become fully hu[ ]
ing citizens."

> —**Darcy Lockman,** author of *All the Rage*

"*Raising Feminist Boys* is an incredibly insightful mélange of history, essential literacy about psychology, parenting realities, and what our society truly needs. It is composed in a genuine voice of a mother, concerned citizen, and a true scholar which speaks to your heart as much as it stimulates your mind. It offers critical questions while offering practical solutions. Our world will be a better place if parents become fluent in the teachings of this book."

> —**Sara Nasserzadeh, PhD,** social psychologist;
> senior cultural advisor to the United Nations;
> cofounder of Relationship Panoramic, Inc.; and
> coauthor of *Sexuality Education Wheel of Context*

"Grounded in scientific research while simultaneously a deeply personal reflection, *Raising Feminist Boys* offers the perfect road map for how we shift the culture of toxic masculinity in the wake of the #metoo movement—beginning with concrete steps we can take in our own homes. As both a clinical psychologist and mother of two young sons, I couldn't be more grateful for this invaluable resource, and for Wegner's insightful (and engaging!) guidance throughout."

> —**Rebecca Schrag Hershberg, PhD,**
> clinical psychologist, parenting coach, and
> author of *The Tantrum Survival Guide*

"Wegner's book is essential for our modern times. Her straightforward approach engages the reader while providing useful strategies which allow boys and their role models to become advocates of equality for all genders. Wegner's authenticity is strengthened by her ability to share her personal challenges with raising her own feminist children. Wegner's sincerity, warmth, and humor give credence to an imperative call to action for change."

—**Katharine "Kim" Larsson, PhD, CNS-BC**, cofounder
of Boston Behavioral Medicine in Brookline, MA;
with over thirty years of experience as a psychotherapist,
psychopharmacologist, consultant, and educator

"Wegner's practical advice guides parents through one of the most important conversations to have during childhood. Having 'the talk' isn't enough if we are to change the toxic culture that persists in society today. The road map provided here starts when our children are young, and these powerful conversations continue throughout their development. This book pushes us to examine our own biases, and provides clear and age-appropriate language to create strong and caring 'feminist boys.'"

—**Elihu Selter, PsyD**, clinical psychologist in private practice,
faculty at the Milton Academy, and father of two sons

"*Raising Feminist Boys* is the guide every parent of boys needs to raise healthy, empathetic sons who contribute in positive ways to society. With the perfect combination of personal stories, practical tips, guided reflection, and evidence, Wegner takes parents by the hand and shows them exactly how to raise feminist boys. Prepare to be comforted by her honesty and inspired by her thoughtful guidance."

—**Erin Erickson, DNP, MPH, MA**, family nurse practitioner;
maternal child health specialist; and cofounder and cohost
of *Mom Enough*, an evidence-based parenting podcast

"Once in a while a parenting book comes along that is rooted in a strong understanding of the best research and thinking about parenting and child development; wise about the nuances of parenting and stocked with concrete, accessible advice and highly practical tips. This is one of those times. I strongly encourage you to read this terrific road map to raising boys who will do the vital work of challenging damaging gender stereotypes in themselves and others, and who will engage in relationships with deep respect and care."

—**Richard Weissbourd**, senior lecturer and faculty
director of the Making Caring Common project at
Harvard Graduate School of Education

"Even the most confident, educated, and well-intentioned parents are struggling to raise their sons—many find ways to talk with their daughters about consent, sex, and equality, but miss out on opportunities to have these critical conversations with their boys. Now there's a remedy: we finally have a book that equips parents and educators with the capacity and confidence to raise a generation of boys as champions of equality. Leaving judgment aside, *Raising Feminist Boys* delivers specific, accessible, and age-appropriate strategies parents can put to use tonight—right at the dinner table."

—**Justine Finn, EdM**, founder and director of Relation-Shift,
consultant to K–12 schools and parents on gender, and mom
grappling with how to raise her own children as feminists

RAISING FEMINIST BOYS

How to Talk with
Your Child about
Gender, Consent & Empathy

BOBBI WEGNER, PSYD

New Harbinger Publications, Inc.

Publisher's Note

Distributed in Canada by Raincoast Books

Copyright © 2021 by Bobbi Wegner
           New Harbinger Publications, Inc.
           5674 Shattuck Avenue
           Oakland, CA 94609
           www.newharbinger.com

Cover design by Amy Shoup

Acquired by Jennye Garibaldi

Edited by Marisa Solís

All Rights Reserved

Library of Congress Cataloging-in-Publication Data

Names: Wegner, Bobbi, author.
Title: Raising feminist boys : how to talk to your child about gender, consent, and empathy / Bobbi Wegner.
Description: Oakland, CA : New Harbinger Publications, Inc., [2021] | Includes bibliographical references.
Identifiers: LCCN 2020052146 | ISBN 9781684036677 (trade paperback)
Subjects: LCSH: Boys. | Child rearing. | Child development. | Feminism. | Moral education. | Personality development.
Classification: LCC HQ775 .W34 2021 | DDC 305.230811--dc23
LC record available at https://lccn.loc.gov/2020052146

Printed in the United States of America

23   22   21

10   9   8   7   6   5   4   3   2   1   First Printing

Contents

Foreword

As a parenting expert and cultural researcher, I deeply believe that the most profound experience we can have as parents is to see ourselves and our world from another perspective. This is where real change happens. This is how a paradigm shift takes place.

So much has changed since we were younger. The tendency many parents have (myself included) is to unwittingly stick our heads in the sand when faced with unfamiliar subjects we aren't well versed in. This isn't anyone's fault. It's typically because we don't know how to tackle certain topics or because anything sex related, gender related, technology related or male privilege related wasn't talked about for most of us growing up.

I am struck by how relevant *Raising Feminist Boys* is to the times we are living in today. As I read, I realized how little I actually knew about what boys are dealing with these days. This book illuminates their experience on so many levels, helping me see the world through my son's eyes, which is one of the biggest takeaways. I have experienced a paradigm shift of my own, and I know a lot of parents will feel the same. I now understand the importance of my role and my husband's role in teaching and modeling the kind of behavior we so desperately need in the world, and this book gives us the tools to do so.

Raising Feminist Boys lifts the veil and shines a light on so many of the different situations and realities our boys are facing nowadays. Oftentimes, they are in the dark with no map to guide them. We need to help our boys develop that strong internal compass that is so necessary to navigate this new terrain toward a better tomorrow. Instead of just saying "no" to difficult topics, let's start saying "know."

There is even a fabulous conversation cheat sheet at the back of this book that I've begun to use in some challenging talks with my son. I liken these conversations to jumping into cold water. It's hard to convince yourself to make the leap initially, it feels a little shocking when you first get in, but once you are there it feels amazing. You feel so glad you did it. I honestly feel closer than ever to my son, and I'm really proud of myself for taking the leap. *Raising Feminist Boys* is just the urging I needed. I can only encourage you to do the same; open this book and dive in!

Dr. Bobbi Wegner is a Harvard clinical psychologist with many years of experience in her practice, and yet, what I love most about this book is her voice throughout the pages. She talks directly to the reader as a parent dealing with their own struggles, offering conversations backed up by science and research. Her humility and humor, combined with the latest information and research, make this book very relatable and real.

Instead of turning away, you will find ways to turn toward opportunities to talk to your son. It can be through the media, technology, or even the music we listen to on the radio. There are so many more possibilities than we realize to open much-needed dialogue in order to guide them into becoming kind, intelligent, and empathic men—what the world needs now more than ever.

—Jessica Joelle Alexander
Author of *The Danish Way of Parenting*:
What the Happiest People in the World Know
About Raising Confident, Capable Kids

Introduction

I woke up to the need for raising feminist boys in the fall of 2017, near the beginning of the #MeToo movement. My then-six-year-old son, Tyler, was lying on the kitchen floor playing Minecraft. I stood at the stove cooking dinner as NPR played in the background. It was a very typical scene in our home.

The radio host was discussing the fallout from allegations that Harvey Weinstein had sexually harassed and assaulted many women, including high-profile actresses. He had been accused of rape and other types of sexual assault, including massaging women and forcing them to look at him naked. When women resisted, he allegedly made threats that ranged from ruining their careers to death.

Around the same time, many other high-profile men were being accused of similar behavior. The NPR host was bewildered at the depth and breadth of the revelations that were pouring out each day. She explored how and why we, as a society, create an environment where we tolerate sexual violence.

Although I was cooking, I was completely absorbed in the horror and absurdity of what I was hearing. As I considered a culture in which one out of every five women has been the victim of an attempted or completed rape, I realized the stats told me that one to two of my daughter's preschool class-mates could be a victim of rape one day! I knew all too well about the deep trauma that sexual violence causes from my work as a clinical psychologist.

My mind wrestled with how a system could so deeply protect sexual predators like Weinstein and others. Every day there had been news of another presumed "good guy" being a pervert. I had even wondered aloud to my husband, *Is this just how guys are wired?* How else could men get away with this for decades? My mind was blown.

Then I remembered that my little guy, with very big ears, was in the room. I dropped the spoon and hustled to turn off the radio when a realiza-tion grabbed me—actually, it was a moment of consciousness. *We are sheltering our developing boys*, I thought. When things are sad, sexual, or uncomfortable, we rush to shield our children in the name of protection, yet who will potentially be hurt by my child's naiveté: A girl in high school? My son himself? Whenever something difficult comes up, we rush to turn off the news or scoot the kids out of the room, and they end up missing out on important conversations as a result.

This thought made me wonder what Harvey's mother had done. What Matt Lauer's father had said. Did Charlie Rose's caregiver ever talk about these things? Despite messaging from the broader culture, what did—or didn't—their parents say when they were little? Think back: Did your caregivers say anything about sexual responsibility when you were six, seven, or eight? If they had said something, would it have changed anything for you? Boys aren't born rapists. So how did guys like these go from being a kid like my loving son to being accused perpetrators? I was suddenly curious about what happened in the time and space in between.

Currently, at nine and eleven years old, my sons Tyler and Cam are in the middle of their cognitive and moral development. As you'll learn in this book, what I say to them actually changes their brain development and will stick with them for a lifetime. The door is wide open, for better or worse; I've got a front-row seat in my boys' prefrontal cortex. My voice matters now, it matters a lot, and in that moment in the kitchen it was clear to me what message I wanted my sons to hear.

So I stepped back to the stove and let the radio play on. I wrung my hands and quietly formulated what to say. Once I found the courage, I said, "Hey, Ty, are you listening to this? This really famous movie guy was saying inappropriate things and touching women when they didn't want to be touched. And now he's in big trouble and there's a good chance he's going to jail."

Then we sat through a long silence. Images of Tyler on the playground butchering the story to his friends flashed before my eyes. I imagined parents calling me and asking, "What the hell are you telling your kid? What the hell is your kid telling my kid?"

Finally, Ty popped his head up and I saw that he wasn't shocked or traumatized. He very matter-of-factly said, "What? Doing that's illegal? Didn't Trump do that?"

I was floored.

I'm not writing this book to make political statements, but I am writing to address the messaging in our communities. In that moment with my son, it became crystal clear to me that I needed to push through the discomfort to bring these topics to the forefront of conversations with my little boys—our future men.

So I said to Ty, "Yeah, Bud, you're right. Trump did say and do inappropriate things, and that is not okay at all. In our family, we do not do that. Ever. Dad doesn't do that. I don't do that. And you are to never do that. Got it?"

"Yes, Mom," he said before going back to the video game. Then he asked, "What's for dinner?"

How Did We Get Here?

The ways we, as parents, need to respond go much deeper than just speaking to our kids about sexual responsibility. Our kids are exposed to a lot of messaging that we likely don't agree with. The messaging gets internalized and becomes part of their developing brains and personalities, shaping their future words and actions. The root of the problems in cultural messaging is gender inequality and how we—particularly boys and men—see our girls and women.

Traditional gender norms are ingrained in childhood and carried into adulthood. Research has found that *benevolent sexism* is prevalent in many men, as they believe things like "Women are better caretakers" or "Women are more people-oriented." Although this is not overt, in-your-face sexism, it affects hiring decisions, how professors are rated, and in what roles women are hired to work (that is, fewer leadership positions).[1] These ideas are somewhat cemented by the age of ten, so early intervention is needed.[2] Aside from shaping gendered behavior, there are health consequences too. When children are more conformative to gender expectations, girls are more depressed, leave school earlier, and are more prone to exposure to violence.[3] Boys engage in more violence, are more prone to substance abuse, and have a shorter life expectancy.[4]

How can we change this for our kids? Foremost, as parents we need to pay attention to our words and actions early in our children's lives. As parents, we are constantly reenacting or reacting to how we were raised. *Reenactment* is when we, consciously or not, follow the ways of our parents, which can perpetuate cultural harms like sexual irresponsibility. *Reacting* is consciously doing something different to create a different result. Parenting the next generation is the most effective agent of social change. This is why we must make a commitment to raise our awareness and react to the traditional gender norms that live within us.

One of my favorite quotes comes from clinical health psychologist George Engel: "Where you think you stand determines what you think you see." If I placed my white American boys in this position, standing in complete privilege, then how could I expect them to see anything outside of that lens?

White male privilege means being able to walk down the street at night and not feel scared or worried that the police are going to stop you. It is going to dinner parties and meetings where your voice is inherently prioritized. It means walking into executive offices and seeing faces that look like yours and hearing words in your comfort zone. It means moving through life without being judged or stereotyped based on your race, gender, or class. It is an invisible invite to the most powerful places.

Entitlement is the frame my boys were handed and the glass through which they see everything. I witness the seedlings of gender inequity budding in my own home despite caring and working to do something different. It's hard to not feel totally screwed and worry that their super-privileged upbringing could result in two more potential future jerks of America. But I—*we*—can have an impact if we focus on our own little humans—they are the next generation, and we have them hostage for eighteen-plus years.

As a white woman who continues to work hard at understanding my own privilege and positioning in the world—and as a psychologist who constantly hears painful stories of assault, discrimination, and misogyny—I want my sons to create an open, loving, accepting culture for all. I know you do too. We know that silence equals violence and that the main weapon in this war is our voice. Let's use it, together.

How This Book Can Help

Make a commitment to raise a *feminist boy*: a feminist boy is a child who believes in equality for all people. He is empathic, self-aware, and perceptive of injustice and inequality in all communities. Feminist boys are willing to speak up and make changes in ways that are developmentally appropriate and within reach.

In this book, you will gain tools to understand your own biases; where your son is in his moral, cognitive, and personality development; and the language as well as a framework for having conversations about empathy, advocacy, kindness, and action. Most important, you will learn ways to raise boys who feel good about themselves. Raising conscious and caring boys who feel understood and cared for is healthiest for them, and also makes them the best allies and advocates for us all.

We are learning alongside each other, so I have created a Reading Group Guide that you can access for free at this book's website, http://www.newharbinger.com/46677, along with other exclusive content. Our personal efforts need to come together for larger societal change.

All of our kids can live consciously, as feminists, with love and understanding for others in their hearts. It is our duty as parents to help them build a solid internal compass and to write a different narrative for the next generation. The best way we can do that is to change the messaging for our kids—especially for our sons.

Join me in exploring our own unique views and connecting what you learn from your own history to what you are teaching your sons. Let's turn toward these issues together. Push through the discomfort, awkwardness, and not knowing—it is all okay and an essential price to pay to create an equitable environment for all. We have a stake in not only raising good men but in shaping the future for ourselves, the country, and the world. Parenting is an agent of social change. Let's make the world a better place through our boys.

CHAPTER 1

Change Starts with You

You probably started the journey into parenthood shooting from the hip or reading books on the logistics of caretaking—what to pack in a diaper bag, how to tell when your kid has a fever, and what the best first food is. Very few people begin their role as a parent focusing on the part that has the most impact: themselves.

If you want to change anything, start with yourself. It then moves to your children, out to your communities, and through generations. We all know this cycle to be true, yet we still expect our kids to "Do as I say, not as I do." Children learn by observing and modeling parents' attitudes, emotional expressions, and behaviors.[5]

Ironically, we still fall into the trap of treating our boys and girls differently, whether consciously or unconsciously. At the core, our tendency to do this perpetuates a culture of gender inequality and sexual violence. Unfortunately, staying away from Barbie dolls and painting everyone's room a gender-neutral color doesn't solve the massive problem. To really make a change in your family and in society, first understand yourself, your own gender bias, and what you are modeling inside and outside the home.

The opportunities for self-reflection in this chapter will help you understand where you are coming from, where you are now, and where you want to go, so you can raise your son more intentionally. Through the power of parental modeling, these insights can move from your own internal world to the larger family dynamic and into society.

To show just how serious I am about this, I invite you to download and sign the Oath of Raising a Feminist Boy. Available as part of this book's online bonus accessories at http://www.newharbinger.com/46677, this oath seals your commitment to doing the hard work outlined in these pages. Because change starts with you.

Modeling Is Not Only Important, It's Inevitable

Our kids are watching and mimicking what we do on a very fundamental, often unconscious level. They see and repeat all of us: the good, bad, and ugly. In families, children watch parents, caregivers, siblings, and extended family to encode and copy what they see. In society, children observe and learn from teachers, coaches, politicians, television characters, media personas, and friends, to name a few. Our kids follow these models regardless of whether their behavior is "positive" or "negative," healthy or harmful, kind or unkind, prosocial or isolationist. Human behavior is shaped by an ongoing and reciprocal relationship between cognitive, social, and behavioral influences.

Most of us embark on the parenting journey using a map that has major holes in it. So we sometimes end up somewhere unintended in Parentland. When that happens—because there's a hole where prior experience should be—we draw from information we already know. This means we pull from the only experiences we have: our memories from childhood and how our parents modeled parenting for us. This may freak you out, as it can sound like you are destined to repeat the childhood you have tried to leave behind. But the good news is that the kind of conscious self-reflection I encourage in this chapter empowers you to *choose* not to repeat the traumas of your past.

Despite our best intentions, it is impossible to control all factors at home, including those that may perpetuate gender roles. For example, the way our family life and work schedules are organized, I am the cook. Always. I enjoy it and I choose to do it, despite knowing my sons and daughter are pairing wives and mothers with cooking.

I am aware of the message I am modeling, yet—as we'll explore later in this chapter—when I notice it, name it, and talk about it, my kids won't assume that women are the only ones who can and should do the cooking for a household.

The initial steps of intentional modeling are:

1. become conscious of the messages you are sending,

2. grow thoughtful about how they match your values, and

3. decide just what you want to instill in your son.

We don't need to parent on autopilot, driven by our own upbringings; instead we can consciously choose what to model so that our boys grow into men who care for and love all people, and who think about women as equals and treat them as such.

The Types of Biases You Might Have

We need to pay attention to our words and actions, but our psychology and socialization can get in our way. One major way we do this is by stereotyping each other based on our biases. My son Ty is obsessed with YouTubers and teen gamers. They are the Elvis and John Lennon of the current culture. And with that comes a certain look, glitz and glam, huge necklaces, and name-brand sneakers. Last week, Ty asked, "Can you take me to get my ears pierced?"

I empathically said, "I know you think that would be so cool, but let's wait until you're a little older. Earrings are permanent and I want you to be older to make that choice."

He quickly and aptly retorted, "You are sexist. If Eve wanted her ears pierced, you would take her."

True. I've actually offered to take my daughter to get her ears pierced multiple times, but she said no because she is scared of the needle. So, being caught in the paradox and feeling unsure, I said, "Okay, I'll think about it."

When we are faced with making decisions, our brains are constantly looking for shortcuts, trying to work as efficiently as possible—it's an evolutionary trait to keep us alive. And because of that, we categorize people—sometimes known as stereotyping—and put them into mental buckets.[6] In this case, I put earrings into the bucket for girls.

Another example of a common bias is that *women are better homemakers and fathers are best suited to work outside the home*. A 200,000-person study done by Harvard from 2005 to 2015 showed that 76 percent of men and women believe that men are better suited for careers and women for homemaking.[7]

When we make assumptions about people, we are creating mental shortcuts. Using the study as an example, if I categorize a woman as "homemaker" and a man as "provider," then I know exactly what to expect from both without ever having to speak with them. I assume she is kind, caretaking, safe, and he is decisive, in control, and driven. The specific adjectives that come to mind are based on our prior experience.

Here are some more common mental buckets: Girls love pink, are sweet, and are fragile. Boys like blue, are active, and are strong. Many say, "Well, boys and girls are just built differently." That is partially true, but brains of men and women are about 90 percent the same,[8] meaning gender roles are mostly socially constructed.

These stereotypes, or biases, come in two forms: implicit and explicit.

Implicit bias: An implicit bias is a stereotype that you don't necessarily realize you hold, or aren't consciously aware of, and do not have conscious control over.[9]

For example, a mother might publicly say that her husband is equally good at parenting, while unconsciously believing she is better solely because she is a woman. Deep down, she might think, *I grew them inside of me, of course I know them better and therefore am a better parent.* That is an implicit bias against men and parenting.

Even people with the best intentions unconsciously do this. Your brain isn't trying to be cruel or unfair, it is trying to be efficient. By using prior information that you have learned from your parents and families, you make assumptions about current information, thereby re-creating their worldview and imposing it on the person or situation in front of you.

Explicit bias: An explicit bias is a stereotype that is conscious and that you know you have.[10]

In my personal example, Ty is right. I am disallowing a behavior—getting ears pierced—solely based on gender. Cut and dry, that is sexist. Ty is a boy, so it is a no for him. Eve is a girl, so it is a yes for her. While this was an implicit bias in me that I had not realized, once Ty pointed it out to me, my continued resistance has become an explicit bias.

Explicit bias is dangerous because people can often perceive and rationalize that these biases are valid, which makes them more likely to justify treating others unfairly and even violently. Explicit biases can be voluntarily activated and presented as deliberate racism and discrimination. The good news is that if something is known, it can also be fought. This takes time and self-reflection; and, while not easy, it can be done.

Because implicit bias is unknown, it has insidious effects. It is called *implicit* because you don't notice it developing. These beliefs form slowly over time based on past lived experiences and attitudes of others around you. Implicit biases can be harmful and dangerous when people subconsciously categorize and stereotype people without pausing to reflect on how accurate those thoughts are, where they came from, and how they may harm others.

It's a brain thing. I encourage you to accept that this happens. Have some self-awareness and self-compassion around it. You are going to have competing feelings. Having self-awareness is what gives you choice in how you respond.

So gain awareness by taking a simple online test created by Harvard University: https://implicit.harvard.edu/implicit/takeatest.html.[11] This test can help unconscious biases become conscious so that you are able to follow the recommendations in this book for working with them. Awareness allows you to make different choices, be mindful of your words, and start conversations with your kids about these things.

After you have taken the test, reflect on the ways implicit gender bias comes up for you. For example, have you ever said or thought, "Men are more physical and more aggressive?" or perhaps "Women are more emotional and dramatic"? Have you ever used gender to excuse a behavior, perhaps saying "Boys will be boys" or "She's just on her period"? That is gender bias, my friend. We put girls in one bucket and boys in another from a very early age.

We don't reconcile this by giving in to simplicity and buying into our bias. Instead, let's recognize that we are complex beings: We can be pro–gender equality *and* sexist at the same time. We can notice our automatic, sexist thoughts *and* make a choice about how to respond. Thoughts are just neural firings—they don't have to become words or behaviors.

Here are some ways to respond after recognizing a gender stereotype at play:

- When your fourth-grade boy says his favorite color is pink, treat him to a new pink stuffed animal to cuddle with.

- Discuss at the dinner table, with your kids present, the negative effects of the whole executive team at work being male.

- Offer horseback riding, dance, and art as extracurricular options to your son, rather than automatically assuming he only wants to play soccer or football.

- Challenge your boy when he says, "That is a girl thing." Ask what makes it so.

- Take on home roles outside of traditional gender jobs: Mom can mow the lawn and coach baseball, Dad can cook dinner, do hair, and treat a scraped knee.

Parenting Is Personal

I often catch myself idealizing my childhood before I remember all the shame and guilt that was also infused in my Irish-Catholic upbringing. That is not what I want for my kids. The way I parent is different than the way I was parented, and that is okay—even healthy—as I adjust to changing norms in a changing world. Today is a different time. Bridging those generational differences and understanding the parenting map I carried over from my childhood is my responsibility to understand. I commit to parenting consciously. I must assess my baggage from childhood and the choice I am making today.

"In the absence of reflection, history often repeats itself, and parents are vulnerable to passing on to their children unhealthy patterns from the past."[12]

To reiterate, much of our childhood experience remains unconscious, yet plays out in our communication, behavior, and emotional expression. For example, we may joke about girls not being as good at math or as strong as boys, because these messages are embedded in us at a deep level. The impact on our children accidentally perpetuates a culture of gender inequality and sexual violence for years to come. This is why self-reflection is not a choice; it is a vehicle of social transformation. In the absence of it, otherwise dated and biased values get unconsciously passed from generation to generation.

How we communicate with our children has a profound impact on their development socially, emotionally, intellectually, and cognitively. Our past doesn't just stay in the past. Of course, there are many factors that contribute to how kids turn out—such as temperament, genetics, physical health, and experience—but what we can control is how we parent. Science tells us that if we get it right about 50 percent of the time, it is "good enough,"[13] meaning we can positively shape the next generation of men.

Research shows that it is not what happened to you that matters most in determining how you raise your children but how you have come to make sense of your early experiences.[14] The goal is to learn about yourself and how you impact your children. Self-understanding helps you parent from a conscious and informed perspective. It promotes a higher mode of processing that is guided by reason, reflective and reciprocal communication, empathy, and morality.[15]

Ty's request for pierced ears really made me think back. I was raised in a conservative Irish Catholic family. When I was young, sayings like "Left is right, right is wrong" helped me make misguided determinations about who was gay based on which ear was pierced. I was also told that having multiple piercings was seen as trashy. (I currently have five of my own piercings, plus a scar from a belly button piercing back in the nineties.) So Ty sees me challenging the norm in some ways and perpetuating a traditional gendered message in other ways. I imagine this is confusing for him, as I know it can feel confusing to me. The remnants of my early messaging are still alive and well in me, although I fundamentally disagree with them too. And that is okay. Acknowledging the paradox and holding both feelings to understand more deeply is what I strive for. I aim for self-reflection without judgment.

Understand Your Bias

The following self-reflection exercises will help you gain a deeper understanding of yourself and the messages you received in your childhood, how they impact your current parenting, and how they can inform where you want to go. The inquiry prompts are divided into themes that tend to reoccur when examining biases such as gender perception, values, emotional expression, division of labor, and roles.

Consider journaling about your past, present, and future goals as a parent. Write openly, freely, and honestly. Be gentle with yourself and go at your own pace. Leave the judgment aside while you chip away at a few prompts at a time. The goal is to raise awareness and link your past to your present. This takes thought, consideration, and time to reflect. Slower is actually better here to give you time to digest.

Exercise 1: Look at Your Past

You likely still hold voices from the past in your head, no matter how much you have learned or changed since then. They can echo through time in your unconscious or conscious mind and influence you—whether you like it or not. The best way to enable choice, for your future and for your son, is to dig into memories and uncover those voices so you can be aware of them. Grab your journal and let's get started.

Gender Perception in General

Think back to your family home or wherever you were raised when you were young. Let your mind go to wherever it goes without getting hung up on age or physical location. Imagine the most important family figures in your life at that moment.

Ask them, "How should a boy behave?" Write down how each family member answers this question. Then write about how each of their messages makes you feel.

Ask them, "How should a girl behave?" Write down how each family member answers this question. Then write about how each of their messages makes you feel.

Sit with this for a moment, without judgment for them or yourself. Just notice the thoughts. Does this messaging align with what you heard about gender from extended family members? From friends? From teachers? Write down your answers.

Explore further: What were the influences behind this messaging? Values, family legacy, religion, cultural heritage, their personal history? What else? Write down your answers.

How Others Perceived Your Gender

Now think of an experience from your childhood when you were aware of your perceived gender (how others saw you). As a boy, did you ever play dress-up with your sister and have your dad come in and tell you that you couldn't wear a skirt because "that's for girls"? As a girl, did anyone ever tell you to act more "ladylike" or to cross your legs when sitting, because girls should be modest? Consider what made you aware of your perceived gender in those moments. Answer these questions in your journal:

- Who was speaking (if anyone)?

- What did you notice?

- What was the messaging?

- How did it make you feel?

- Were you supported or denied?

- How would it feel to be different than how you were perceived in that moment?

- Was that message congruent with other messages you got in childhood about gender and how to act?

Values

Think back to an early childhood memory. Don't judge. Just see where your memory lands. Answer these questions in your journal to go more deeply into what it was like growing up.

- What adjectives come to mind to describe this experience (sad, happy, discouraging, supportive, angry, disappointing, and so on)?

- Which family members were in the memory?

- What family values were being expressed?

- In general, what were your family's top three values?

- Did gender influence or impact these values? If so, how?

- What did your mother really want you to value? Your father? Other primary caregivers?

- What was your relationship like with your mother or mother figure? How about with your father or father figure? Were they similar or different? Did gender influence your relationship with either?

Emotional Expression

Think back to your family home or wherever you were raised when you were young. Let your mind wander without getting hung up on age or physical location. Imagine the most important family figures in your life at that moment. Notice how emotion was expressed in your home.

- Was emotion expressed or suppressed?

- How did your family members show they were angry, sad, happy, and excited?

- How did you know they were feeling this way?

- Was your family an emotionally expressive family? If so, how did that affect you? If not, what did this teach you about your emotions?

- How were different emotions received? For example, how was your sadness approached? Anger?

- Would your mother and father respond similarly or differently to your emotions? In what ways did they respond?

- Did gender influence how emotions were expressed, received, discouraged, or tolerated for you and your siblings? If so, how? Why do you think you were treated differently?

Division of Labor and Roles

Picture a typical activity in your childhood home environment, just notice without judging yourself or anyone else. Observe. Be curious about why people are doing what they are doing. In your journal, write or draw what you notice.

- Where is everyone?

- What is your mother doing? Your father? Grandmother? Sister? Brother? Aunt? Uncle? Cousins?

- Are they acting according to gender expectations?

- Are women acting in typical female roles (cooking, cleaning, watching the children, serving, sewing, soothing, keeping peace)?

- Are the men acting according to male stereotypes (grilling, mowing, fixing things around the house or on the car, making decisions, punishing, playing or watching sports)?

- Are the activities their choice?

- Who is calling the shots?

- Did anyone want to do something different? If so, who? Why didn't they?

- How did gender expectations impact everyone's activities?

Exercise 2: Building Self-Awareness of the Present

Have you ever caught yourself in an unexpected moment responding to your kids in a certain way and thought, *Wow, I sound just like my mother?* Maybe you fought your whole teenage years to be anything *but* like your mom, and yet here you are sounding just like her. In this exercise we'll explore the ways your childhood, your parents' values, and the family gender roles you witnessed growing up affected and shaped your present view of the world.

Impact of Childhood

It's time to reflect on how your childhood has affected your adult life. Whether we like it or not, our past has shaped our present. In order to move forward, we must face our past and really ask ourselves some difficult questions. In your journal, write or draw answers to these questions.

- Has your childhood affected your life positively? Negatively? Both? In what ways?

- How have childhood experiences shaped your parenting perspective, whether positively or negatively or both?

- Do you parent according to your expectations? If so, how? If not, what has influenced you otherwise?

- Do you think you would parent differently if you were of a different gender?

- What values have you brought with you into your adult life from childhood?

- What are the top three values you want to instill in your child? Why these three?

- Did you learn these values during your childhood?

- Are you actively instilling them in your child now? If so, how? If not, what influenced you differently?

- Consider whether these values apply differently to sons and daughters. Are these values gender-dependent? If so, how?

Family Values of Gender

Think about your child and family. Let your mind go to wherever it goes without getting hung up on age or physical location. Then respond to these prompts in your journal.

- How do you believe a boy should behave?

- How do you believe a girl should behave?

- What do you think about these beliefs? How do you feel about the similarities and differences in how you expect children to act?

- How do you communicate these beliefs to your child verbally and nonverbally?

- Do you believe there are any things boys shouldn't do? Girls? Why might you place these limitations on their behavior?

Reflect and notice. Sit with this for a moment, without judgment. Observe your thoughts and feelings. Write them down.

- Does your messaging align with what you want for your child?

- Are you sending different messages to your son and your daughter, or your niece and nephew? Or are your expectations for them the same?

- How does this messaging align with what your child is hearing from friends, school, family, community, culture, religion? What are other important influences on your son's life?

- Are there things you want to change about what you are communicating to your child? If so, what?

Now think of an experience when you were aware of your son's gender. (Feel free to also repeat these questions for a daughter, if you have one.) Maybe it was when someone thought your son was a girl simply because he had long hair. Perhaps it was something someone said or the way someone acted differently around your child due to his gender.

- Who was speaking (if anyone)?

- Did you notice anything? What was the messaging?

- How did it make you feel?

- Was your child's gender supported or denied?

- Was anyone else being singled out as being different or not part of a group?

- Was this message congruent with the general messaging your kid gets in his life about gender and how to act?

- How did this interaction align with your values and what you want for your child?

- If it didn't, is there something you could have said to change this for your son? If so, what?

Now let's add on to that and think about your relationship with your son. (Again, feel free to repeat these questions for a daughter.)

- What is your relationship like with your son?

- What is your partner's relationship like with your son?

- Are they similar or different? Why? Is it influenced by gender? If so, how? Why?

- Is there anything you would want to do to make it more equitable?

- How do you think this impacts your relationship with your child and partner now and in the future?

Values and Emotional Expression

Think about your current family and home environment.

- Who is included in your family (for example, grandparents, nannies, close friends)?

- What are your family values?

- What would your son say if you asked him to name the three most important family values?

- Are those the same or different than what you named as the most important family values?

- Are the family values consistent across all family members or do they vary by person? If so, how do they differ and why?

- How is emotion expressed in your home? Is emotion expressed?

- What kinds of emotions are easier for you to handle?

- What emotions create an emotional response in you? What feelings are hardest for you to manage? Why?

- How do you know if someone is angry, sad, happy, or excited in your family?

- How do you know when someone is expressing emotion?

- Would you say your family is an emotionally expressive one?

- How do you receive emotion? Do you become sad, angry? Do you and your partner respond similarly or differently to your emotions? In what way?

- Is there anything you would like to do differently to show that all emotion is good emotion and is openly welcomed by your son?

- Do you think your son hears the same messaging from you and your partner about emotional expression?

Division of Labor and Roles

Who are the most important family figures in your son's life now? Name them. Pick a typical scene in your home. Just notice without judging yourself or anyone else. Observe. Be curious why people are doing what they are doing.

- Where is everyone?

- What is everyone doing? Mom? Dad? Nanny? Grandmother? Sister? Brother? Aunt? Uncle?

- Are women in typical female roles? How about the men?

- Is it their choice?

- Who is calling the shots?

- What message is being nonverbally communicated to your child?

- Is this in line with your values and what you want your child to know and think?

- Is there room for improvement? If so, how?

Exercise 3: Prioritize What You Want in the Future

Looking at your past isn't always comfortable. We can unearth aspects of ourselves we've been spending years trying to forget, trying to believe they aren't a part of us. Fortunately, by doing the hard work of looking squarely at your past, you're able to better guide your and your family's future in the direction you want.

So now, let's sit with your reflections of your past and present. Think through your answers or write them in your journal.

- What jumps out to you? What have you learned about yourself?
- What has been most meaningful? Why?
- If you fast-forward ten years, how do you picture yourself?
- What do you look like? Where you are? Who are you with?

Now picture your son. And any other children. Add ten years to them today.

- How do you see them?
- What kind of people do you want them to be?
- How can you foster empathy in them today to create empathic people in the future?
- How can you foster equality today to create a sense of equality in them in the future?
- How can you teach listening and connection to promote positive, healthy relationships for them in the future?
- What needs to change now to align your future hopes with your present?

Pick three family values you want to prioritize in your family. Repeat them three times. Focus on them. Think through how to integrate them daily, weekly, and yearly. What can you do to start today?

By doing these exercises, you're helping reshape your family's future by ensuring that conscious, self-reflective, and deliberate thoughts and actions are guiding your family's values and trajectory going forward.

Parenting in Partnership at Home

It is so important to self-reflect and tie your own history to how you are raising your family *and* that you don't parent in isolation. Although you can't control all the messaging your son absorbs, you and your partner can be clear about your messaging together, which often holds the most weight. Being on the same page as a team is much healthier for your child, whether it is about feminism or something else.[16] If you want to raise a son who believes in and promotes equality, it is super important to make the message clear and consistent across parents. Some of this might include teaching your partner what *feminism* is—a belief in equality for all.

The details of how boys (and girls) should be raised evokes more conflict than one might assume in this current day and age. A common scenario is a dad who says, "Yes, of course I believe in equality for my kids" but at the same time calls his daughter "Princess" and makes it clear to the family that she should be prized. Or a mom who says, "Yes, I treat my kids the same" but pushes her son to play sports "like the other boys." Comments like these are well intentioned but considered *microaggressions:* subtle comments that communicate bias. In these examples, the bias is on gender roles.

Microaggressions are also made more explicit in how parents choose (consciously or not) to divide labor among themselves. Gendered messaging isn't just what you say to someone else, it is what you show in your own behavior. In couples, this comes up with division of labor—work inside and outside of the home—and who does what, when, and how much.

Division of Labor

Parenting in partnership doesn't mean equality in the way you might assume. It is impossible for partners to carry equal amounts of each load. Each family has a unique set of demands, and every family is organized differently, almost always with one partner earning more money than the other, and with one partner taking primary responsibility for the tasks associated with raising the kids.

Parenting in partnerships means having honest, ongoing conversations with your partner about the various needs of the family: caretaking of the kids, caretaking of the marriage, caretaking of the finances, caretaking of external family and friends, and so on.

Many women find themselves naturally leaning into the caretaking role while conversely feeling resentful that they "do it all." Of course, it *feels* natural in part because women (and men) have been primed by our culture to believe that women do kids better than men. Your tendency to fall prey to this type of culturally prescribed message should be challenged. One way to do this is to step back from your assumed roles, look consciously at who does what, and make choices about how to divide labor in a way that feels equitable to you and your partner. It also allows both of you to be more engaged in and motivated by shared goals, rather than by following an unconscious cultural script.

Open, honest communication about shared responsibilities not only feels better as a couple and minimizes resentment that often builds over the years, it also models for your child how work is shared, regardless of your gender. When you are always the first to rush to respond to your baby, or the first to hop up to do the dishes, or the last one home from work, or always the one to discipline, be conscious of what motivates you. You are sending a message to your boy about who does what. Raising feminist boys means conscious parenting and conscious sharing of labor.

Divvy Up Responsibilities

When both you and your partner are in a good headspace, sit down together and make a comprehensive list of all the demands of your home. Then indicate who does what and how often. You can also visit this book's website at http://www.newharbinger.com/46677 to download the Division of Labor Check-In form, a free resource designed to help you and your partner get a clear sense of how you're really dividing responsibilities.

Traditional Beliefs in a Modern World

If you feel stuck between your progressive beliefs and the reality of your life, especially when it comes to the division of labor, you're not alone. The first step is to understand the impact of where you came from and where we are as a culture today.

First, the good news:

- Men today are more consciously committed to creating an equal relationship at home, which includes cooking dinner, taking care of the kids, and participating in chores that have been historically designated "women's work."[17]

- Men want an egalitarian relationship.[18]

- Men are, in fact, doing more than they used to.[19]

The bad news is that even in families where both parents work outside of the home (46 percent of families),[20] how the work is divided remains imbalanced, although the men don't see it that way (but the data says otherwise). Women are still absorbing more of the childrearing and chores while *also* working outside of the home. Interestingly, men feel like the housework is more balanced than what the women report and what the research shows. In the couples' counseling world, this is a common point of contention.

Don't blame it all on the men though. Research has found that persistently gendered workplace norms and policies affect men and women's ability to create an egalitarian home. So if we want real change, we have to change the community in which we live.[21] But let's start with the home.

So, people, the short answer is that if you want to have a truly balanced and equitable home environment, the chores have to be shared more. This will pay dividends in your kitchen, your parenting, and bonus—in your bedroom. Couples who report more egalitarian divisions of routine housework have more sex.[22] So how do we get there?

Sit down together and make a list of all the housework. Use the list from the previous exercise as a starting point. Remind yourself that a fifty-fifty balance is not the goal and is impossible. Instead, the aim should be on creating a mutually agreed upon fair division of labor. Both partners have to come to terms with the fact that a tit-for-tat approach ruins relationships. Keep in mind that housework is a moving target and changes over time as children grow, work schedules shift, and life changes. Reevaluate where you are with this every six months or so.

As you start this communication, both partners have to give up some control. This is often the hardest, as couples have usually already established their roles and spheres of household influence, or lack of influence, or are set on a particular way they want things done. It is important in this process to communicate honestly and to commit to not managing the other's tasks.

Sure, you wish your partner would really scrub the bathtub grout the way you do, but you will have to give a little and realize in the end that they did clean the bathroom even if it wasn't totally up to your standards. Honest communication is the best weapon against relationship discord, and how you divide labor is no different. Your partner isn't a mind reader as much as you might like to believe they should just "get it." Communicate honestly, openly, and thoughtfully.

Family Work

Don't just involve your partner in the household chores—get your kids on board too! Research from a well-known, long-term study at Harvard showed that kids who had chores did better later in life: they were happier, healthier, and more independent.[23] Family work is also a way for children to both contribute to the household in a meaningful way and get comfortable doing work that is "family work" rather than gendered tasks.

If your son has been doing his laundry his whole life, he is less likely to think of laundry as women's work when he is older. He will just see it as self-care and self-preservation. Prioritize the idea that "everyone contributes," and be careful not to assume jobs and responsibilities just because you might feel that you do it better, faster, or because it is caretaking. By stepping in, you are not only depriving your son of developing healthy life skills, you are also unintentionally teaching him that laundry is for parents (or women) to do for others, which in turn he will unconsciously build into his developing brain.

Here are lists of common household tasks your child can likely handle depending on age:

Chores for Kids Ages 2 to 4

- Put dirty laundry in the hamper
- Fold clean laundry
- Put away toys
- Clean up the mess before leaving any room, the bathtub, and so forth
- Help clear the kitchen table
- Help set the table
- Sweep
- Wipe down counters
- Put away some dishes
- Feed the animals
- Make the bed

Chores for Kids Ages 5 to 10

- Make the bed every day
- Brush own teeth and hair
- Dress self
- Clean a room, including picking up items off the floor and vacuuming
- Unload the dishwasher
- Make a small purchase at a store while parent is in car
- Help prep dinner
- Set the dinner table
- Clear the table after dinner
- Pick up toys from the yard
- Help a parent with yardwork
- Shovel snow or rake leaves
- Take out the trash

Chores for Kids Ages 11 to 13

- Keep track of own stuff
- Get self up in the morning
- Strip the bed and wash the sheets once a week
- Keep room clean and organized
- Be responsible for cleaning one room a week (other than the bedroom)
- Prepare dinner sometimes
- Mow the lawn
- Babysit
- Shovel snow, rake leaves, or help an elderly neighbor
- Walk to the store

Chores for Kids Ages 14+

- Manage own day-to-day responsibilities, such as homework, schedule, and hygiene
- Do yard work
- Clean one room a day (not full cleaning)
- Babysit
- Prepare meals periodically
- Grocery shop
- Shuttle sibling to practices, if needed

School as Community

We have to remember that, in many ways, our kids' ecosystems are very small. Yes, they are online and have friends, but the main drivers of information and education (especially when they are young) are home and school. While we can't control modeling happening at school, we can help encourage changes in our broader community that could positively affect the modeling our boys receive.

The best way to effect a change is to collaborate with the school and community around you. A collaborative approach is always most fruitful, at least at the beginning. A very wise teacher once told me, "Always go in like a lamb and then you have room to become a lion, if necessary." What your son sees in all facets of his life shapes his belief system. Here are questions to think about and ask concerning gender equity in the classroom:[24]

What is the ratio of male to female teachers?

What subjects are taught, whose histories are told, and through whose lens and values? Whose voices aren't being heard?

Are there about equal numbers of boys and girls in all classes?

What is the prevalence of reported harassment by boys and girls? What is being reported?

How is the school gendered? When are boys and girls segregated? Why? How? When?

Where is the school system spending money? Is it about equal across activities associated with one gender versus another?

What is the tone of gender at school? Are all kids encouraged to play and work together? How is that explicitly communicated? What is implicitly felt by students, staff, and family?

Has the school formally explored gender equity via survey, interview, or another measure? If so, how? If not, why?

Harvard Graduate School of Education's Making Caring Common (MCC) offers concrete programming to be implemented in schools for building equity and for the common good of everyone at school.[25] Encourage your school to implement MCC's programming and follow its lead.[26]

For a complete and thorough resource on building a family-school-community partnership, check out *The Power of Family School Community Partnerships: A Training Resource Manual,* from the National Education Association's Priority Schools Campaign.[27] To begin, though, ask questions. Volunteer to read and do projects on equity. Talk with your son's friends about equity and feminism, and maybe they will start to talk about it at school.

Raising a feminist son means pushing equity in all parts of his (and your) life. This is not a battle that will be won overnight, it is one that takes consistent and frequent attention across all domains over time.

Feminist Takeaways

Self-reflection is not a choice; it is a vehicle of social transformation. Many parents feel the daunting responsibility of making the world an equitable place but don't know how. Acceptance of our own history and messaging must happen before any change can occur. Self-reflection allows an acknowledgment of the history we internalized while offering an opportunity to do something different. In the absence of it, otherwise dated and biased values get unconsciously passed from generation to generation.

Everyone carries the weight of the gendered messages we received as kids and from culture. You learned what that is for you and how it plays out in your home now. You also made a plan for integrating a more equitable environment in your home. The next chapter will help you take your ideas and apply them to your son, wherever he might be in his own developmental stage.

CHAPTER 2

Understand Developmental Stages and Strategies

White boys raised with middle to high socioeconomic status need to be tasked with acknowledging the privilege they breathe and with consciously resisting the cultural messaging that tells them it is okay to take what they want, whenever they want. When they are surrounded by men who look like they do and have a sense of entitlement, if one of them behaves badly or takes advantage—and gets away with it—our sons will think they can too. This has enormous social cost. They aren't going to just get up one day in college, totally woke, and get it. Thinking back to my college days at frat parties, the vibe of "anything goes" depending on your skin color and socio-economic status was accepted as the unspoken law of the land. I wish this had changed over time, but, from my patients, I know much has not.

So it is our responsibility to raise the next generation of potential frat boys in a way that is kind, caring, and empathic. We must look honestly at our sons' positioning in the world, understand them and the culture they are in, and find language to build conscientious and respectful boys—one conversation at a time. It is our job now, as parents raising young men, to instill awareness, compassion, and empathy as they build their internal frameworks.

There are developmental theories that can help you discern what is appropriate to communicate with your boys and when. In this chapter, I draw on these theories to offer concrete recommendations for the stage your son is in or will soon pass through. Of course, all our stories, families, and histories are different. Culture, gender, race, age, other demographic variables, and their intersections shape the world in which your boy lives, but there are certain truths that can guide you. Going back to the theories that show what is developmentally appropriate and effective can always be your grounding force and a great place from which to start.

It is crucial to name the unique challenges your son faces. The way I speak to my sons about assumptions people might make about them will be different than the way you speak. Use your judgment and trust that you know best. There is not a one-size-fits-all framework, and certain populations will face different obstacles, which is explained by *intersectionality*.

Intersectionality is the interconnected nature of social categorizations such as race, class, sexuality, ability, gender, physical appearance, and more. These create overlapping and interdependent systems of privilege, entitlement, discrimination, or disadvantage,[28] which affects our boys in different ways. For example, although being male is thought of as a privilege, not all males have the same and equal privilege. Men of color face far more discrimination, especially if they are of low socioeconomic status or have intellectual disabilities, and our culture has a legacy of bias against Black men in rape accusations.[29] The white boys might be perpetrating (and getting away with it), but the boys of color are being accused.[30]

I encourage all parents to think about how intersectionality affects your son, how you parent, and what you communicate to your son. There isn't one go-to canned conversation I can hand you. The real work is sitting with your own discomfort and anxiety, and pushing through to have any conversation. My clinical experience has shown that shaming and negative associations around sexuality in childhood affect people well into adulthood and impact self-worth, choice of partners, mental health, sexual identity, and how we see ourselves in the world. Help your boy by being straightforward about sharing information about gender and sex.

You're reading this book because you care. Let's collectively put our heads together and make a difference, trusting your own knowledge of both yourself and your son.

Don't Delay Conversations

Communication has a lasting impact on our boys, especially affecting their sexual development and behavior.[31] Good sex education and communication, including skills-based knowledge, is an effective strategy for preventing sexual assault, and it has to start early.[32] Earlier than we are currently doing and potentially earlier than you are comfortable with. Trust that saying something is better than saying nothing and that it is never too early to start. Talking with kids about sexuality isn't going to make them have sex earlier. In fact, children who know more about this topic tend to wait to have sex until they are older and use contraceptives when they do eventually have sex.[33]

While I am sure you know the value of speaking with your kids about these issues, and want to say something that is effective, you may not know what to say—so instead, you avoid it.[34] Parents often fear not knowing how to have these conversations or think their children are too young. Make emotional, sensible, reciprocal, and informed communication the goal. Research shows the factors that make these conversations easiest include:

- When there is a good parent-child relationship

- When parents capitalize on (rather than avoid) spur-of-the-moment opportunities to talk about sex

- When conversations started when the kids were young

If these conversation topics are just part of the fabric of your lives together, there is no discomfort. Realize this is your own discomfort, not your young son's. This is a "you thing" not a "him thing." For him, sex education has not yet been shrouded in awkwardness, silliness, and discomfort. Instead it is more about understanding how our bodies work, why they work that way, and what that looks like. It can feel normal and casual, if you start the conversation early enough.

Before we can get the words out, it is important to know what words to use. Understanding how the words might be received gives us perspective on what to say. To communicate in a way that is connecting and educational rather than uncomfortable and awkward, we can apply *cognitive, psychosocial,* and *moral theory* to know how to address where our boys are in their personal development.

Stages of Cognitive Development

Cognitive development theorist Jean Piaget believed that children are much like little scientists, making observations, testing new ideas, and learning as they go. Kids engage with their environment, build off what they already know, and adjust their thinking as new information is learned. For example, a child sees the stove. He is interested in the shape and color, and reaches to touch it. After a burn, he retracts. The parent says "hot," and now the child accommodates the new information, understanding that the stove creates pain and is called "hot."

In terms of sexual development, the approach is much the same. In the introduction, I shared the story of how Ty had absorbed the message from our culture that it is okay to touch women when they don't want to be touched because President Trump did that. When I just happened to stumble upon him thinking this, I had to pause, give new information, and help his little mind accommodate it to create a new belief. This type of learning becomes more sophisticated as a person ages and builds upon more complicated information, but the process is very much the same.

It makes all the difference to build the foundation of a house properly rather than trying to do it once all the walls are up. Same with a developing brain. Let's look at the developmental stages Piaget identified with the intention of getting closer to developmentally appropriate wording and concepts.

Sensorimotor Stage: Birth to 2 Years Old[35]

Your little drooling nugget isn't just cute, he is actually going through a major phase of dramatic growth and learning in a relatively short period of time. He's at ground zero for cognitive development, and it's directly impacted by parents and caregivers. His knowledge is built upon the sensory experiences we offer, opportunities to play and manipulate objects, and the language that is heard. What you input is the foundation on which he builds his cognition.

Babies understand the world through their movements and sensations:

- Their main vehicle of learning is through basic actions such as sucking, grasping, looking, and listening.

- They develop "object permanence" or "object constancy," which means they understand that objects exist even when they aren't seen (for example, "I have a mother, although she isn't here right now").

- They begin to understand that they are separate from the people and objects around them, rather than being an extension.

- They realize cause and effect (for example, "If I cry, then Dad will pick me up").

- They develop representational thought, which is the ability to hold an idea, image, or thought in their mind (for example, "ball" is the round, soft thing they played with this morning).

So how do you *model*, or talk about, things like gender, consent, and empathy with a toddler? Consider his environment to be the ground from which he learns. If it is inequitable and unempathic, he is building cognitive models in his mind that represent that. If Mom is always the one to respond to the baby when he cries, the baby starts to learn Mom is the one who responds. Over time, this becomes unconsciously tied to gender. I'll discuss this more later, but at this stage it's important to think of all the chores that are often gendered. Maybe Mom does the laundry, Dad mows the lawn, Mom cooks, and Dad coaches sports. Aside from personal beliefs, these behaviors are teaching the child about how the world works, what they should do, and what they should expect of others.

Our children are absorbing language all around them. Be conscious of the language you use and the messages you send. Too often girls are sent the message that they need to be pretty, act demurely, or should apologize first. Boys are given the message that they're supposed to be rough, in charge, and don't need help.

Think of these early years as a training period for you to get comfortable with talking about these things before your kid is old enough to be awkward about it. This is your sex education training camp. Practice talking with your baby. He will love the engagement and smile back—what positive reinforcement for you!

Preoperational Stage: 2 to 7 Years Old[36]

Kids at this younger age range do not hold gender constant—they don't maintain a constant identification of an object or person with changing appearances.[37] However, around age five to six years old, gender constancy starts to take place and what they have learned about social expectations around gender becomes concretized. Here are ways that they're developing:

- They're looking and listening.

- Language development is occurring.

- They continue to develop symbolic thinking (that is, playing "family" and role-playing).

- They are focused on self-mastery.

- They think without logical rules or concrete thoughts.

- They have *egocentric thought*, or an inability to see other people's perspectives.

- They do not understand conservation yet (for example, a tall and skinny glass of water can hold the same volume as a short and wide glass).

How kids think affects how gendered information is understood, processed, and responded to, meaning they start to make assumptions about how they and others should act based on gender. It is therefore important that parents recognize this and challenge the gendered roles that are automatically absorbed from the culture in which they live (such as the home, school, and broader community).

When Ty, at age six, said, "Those are girl sneakers and I don't want to wear them," I didn't oppose, rather I questioned why. "What makes them girl sneakers? How do you know that? Where do you think you learned that? What would happen if a boy wore them? Dad thinks they are cool and he is a guy." Not only does this approach challenge developing cognitive models, it also raised his awareness and gave language to use outside of the home when these topics arise.

In my house, I always use the garden as a metaphor for sex. "You know how we plant a seed and a tomato plant grows? Getting pregnant is very much like that. Men have seeds they put in the woman by putting his penis in her vagina, and the seed mixes with the woman's egg to make a baby. This is one way to make a baby and there are others we can talk about later."

Of course, this is an oversimplified version of explaining reproductive sex to a little boy, but it is a starting point. Start with what is most relevant to your son. In my home, my husband and I are cisgender, straight, and in a monogamous marriage. How I got pregnant is where I am starting from. There are many modern ways that people make families and have babies now—for example, through in vitro fertilization, with donor sperm, with two moms or two dads, or through adoption—and it is important to share those as well. Once my son understood how he got into the world, we moved on to how other families have babies and talked about it in a similar, matter-of-fact way.

Concrete Operational Stage: 7 to 11 Years Old[38]

During this stage, children's thinking becomes more sophisticated. It is the bridge between the young days of simple, concrete thought to older, more abstract thinking. The movement away from egocentricism is the hallmark of this stage, and kids in this age group can now understand that others have differing views. They now solve problems using logic and apply concrete skills.

- They develop more sophisticated, logical ways to sort out abstract thoughts (for example, "I don't feel well every time I drink milk, so I won't drink milk anymore").

- Egocentricism is eliminated. They learn that people can have other views than they have.

- Awareness of reversibility develops (for example, "A Honda is a type of car and a type of car is a Honda").

- Kids begin to understand conservation. Although the shape of a container changes, the amount of the liquid inside remains the same (for example, pouring a tall, skinny glass of water into a short, wide mug doesn't change the amount of water although it might look different).

- They hold many different parts of a problem at once (for example, "I want to go to the party. I also want to go to hockey. My mom wants me to visit Grandma. Hmm, what to do?").

So, what do you need to know in terms of communicating with your seven- to eleven-year-old boy? In my home, this looks like two boys asking questions about sex that aren't attached to much meaning for them. They know it is a little awkward, since they have come to learn that sex is a topic they can speak with me about but that it isn't appropriate to talk about in all contexts.

My ten-year-old son and I were driving when a song came on the radio and mentioned lesbians. In an open, curious manner, Cam asked how two women make a baby. I explained the options: "They can adopt, get a 'sperm seed' from a doctor who implants it in one of the women, or the doctor can mix the sperm and the egg and implant it in another woman who carries the baby for the couple. The same ingredients are necessary but the way in which they are mixed and implanted differ depending on the couple."

The conversation was simple and straight to the point. Teaching sex through the garden metaphor—you plant a seed in a fertile garden and beautiful tomatoes will grow in the right conditions—helps concretize sex and pregnancy for children early on and allows them to build off the basic science they know to ask questions.

Most recently, Cam, after watching YouTube asked, "What does it mean to not drop the soap in the jail shower?" Although my internal reaction was a bit shocked, I broke it down into parts and asked what he knew about. "Do you know what sex is? Do you know about gay sex? Rape? Trauma?" are a few questions I started with. If you are jumping out of your skin thinking about these questions, ask yourself: *Is this* my *response or my son's?* How do you know that these questions are uncomfortable? What makes them uncomfortable? Is there a way for you to not feel so queasy saying them to your son?

Formal Operational Stage: 12 to Adulthood[39]

By age twelve, kids develop the ability to think abstractly, hold multiple points of view, solve problems, and think with more sophistication. This sounds all well and good, but in terms of neuropsychological development, their frontal lobes (which are responsible for high-level thinking) are not fully developed until age twenty-five.

- They develop abstract and theoretical concepts.

- They use logic to creatively solve problems.

- Deductive reasoning, logic, and organized planning emerges.

The conversation around sex, empathy, and consent is a must by this age. However, many parents wait too late to talk with their kids about these issues because they haven't laid the groundwork in years prior. Although your boy's cognition and social awareness is more developed by this stage, the meaning he absorbed from the culture is already embedded, so you might be competing against his embarrassment.

If you have not begun sex conversations, you aren't screwed, but it is worth acknowledging to your son that you wish you had brought this up earlier. You could say something like, "I waited until you were older to talk about sex because that is what my parents did, but part of me wishes we had started talking about this sooner. All I want you to know is that I'm here. I'm comfortable with any and all of your questions, and I'm happy we can talk together now. What are your questions? More questions will come up later, and it is always okay to ask me."

Development in a Social World

Lev Vygotsky believed parents, caregivers, and culture play a huge part in developing children's cognition, and that social factors greatly shape what children learn.[40] His theory is important because it highlights how our community shapes our sons much more than we might appreciate. For example, you may have rules in your home (such as no YouTube) but your son's friends may have different rules and therefore access to different, often mature knowledge. According to this sociocultural theory:

- Development of cognition occurs in a cultural context.

- Language plays a huge role in how cognition develops.

- Unlike Piaget, there are no stages of development.

All learning is filtered through the social context in which a child lives. How the child thinks is directly linked to the people and messaging around him. Pay attention and consider the sociocultural context your son is in—this informs his development regardless of your belief system.

Our boys live in a social world and they will be exposed to things well beyond their years. Assume this, then block and tackle with conversation, collaboration, sharing, and education. Don't live in the dark.

We need to pay attention to what we are saying, what we (personally and culturally) are inputting, and think about how it impacts our sons' cognition. At six years old, Ty learned from President Trump that it was okay to touch women when they don't want to be touched. He did not receive that message from my husband or me, he absorbed it from the culture at large, unbeknownst to us.

We often assume we have control over what kids are learning, but the reality is that they are their own little beings living in a social world that is molding who they are. While our kids are shaped by the cultural world around them, our willingness to talk about it puts it in context. We can either watch on the sidelines or be an active participant in conversation with them as they go.

Stages of Psychological Growth

Psychosocial development is personality development that is influenced by social, cognitive, emotional, and behavioral factors.[41] Erik Erikson theorized that personality is developed by successfully mastering eight interdependent stages that are marked by different psychological struggles. After successful completion of one stage, the person moves on to the next, more sophisticated stage.

What follows is a simple overview of a commonly cited psychosocial development theory. For our purposes, it is important to understand where you son is in terms of his psychological struggle and what he needs to achieve. This helps filter for more effective communication by knowing your audience. Here are the stages[42] with theory translated into practice.

Stage I: Birth to 18 months

Psychological struggle: Trust versus mistrust

Life event: Feeding

Outcome: If caregivers appropriately respond to their needs, children learn that the world is responsive. If not, they develop mistrust.

What to talk about: Talking about sex should happen before they are verbal. Use appropriate terms for genitals to set the tone of comfort around talking about sexuality.

Stage II: 2 to 3 years old

Psychological struggle: Autonomy versus shame and doubt

Life event: Toilet training

Outcome: Children learn physical control over themselves and develop autonomy. If not, then shame and doubt ensue.

What to talk about: Start talking about consent, boundaries, and bodies. You are setting the tone for future conversations and giving language.

Stage III: 3 to 5 years old

Psychological struggle: Initiative versus guilt

Life event: Exploration

Outcome: They learn to assert control over their environment and develop a sense of initiative. If they are too controlling, the feedback they get causes guilt.

What to talk about: Talk about gender differences, consent, and body talk should continue.

Stage IV: 6 to 11 years old

Psychological struggle: Industry versus inferiority

Life event: School

Outcome: Children learn to adapt to new demands in the social world (friends and school) and develop industry. Failure to do so creates inferiority.

What to talk about: Sexual safety—including abuse—safe touching, masturbation, erections, menstruation, the mechanics of sex, puberty, gender expression, objectification of women, sexism, internet safety, safe sex, STDs, media, and pornography are all fair game.

Stage V: 12 to 18 years old

Psychological struggle: Identity versus role confusion

Life event: Social relationships

Outcome: Teens separate from parents and develop a sense of self outside the family, which fosters identity development. Failure to do so creates role confusion.

What to talk about: Consent, emotions, healthy relationships, safe sex, good choices, following one's internal compass, self-awareness, empathy toward others, and language are good topics of discussion. Act as a consultant in making good choices.

Stage VI: 19 to 40 years old

Psychological struggle: Intimacy versus isolation

Life event: Intimate relationships

Outcome: Young adults develop close, intimate, loving relationships that result in intimacy. Failure to do so creates isolation.

What to talk about: Gears switch here for many parents (though not all, especially if you have a son with intellectual disabilities, for example). Parents shift roles but can continue to be a resource in college and beyond in helping their boys make good judgments around relationships, understanding themselves in relationships, healthy behaviors, life choices, and generally making conscious choices rather than following the herd. Parents might share more about personal, lived experiences during this stage too.

Cultivating Moral Development

Now that you know Jean Piaget's cognitive theory, I want to introduce you to his theory of moral development. He was not interested in the choices children make but how children think about morality—an extension of his cognitive theory, so to speak.[43] The take-home point for any modern parent is that children's ideas regarding rules, moral judgments, and punishments change over time and include two types of morality: *heteronomous* (moral realism) and *autonomous morality* (moral relativism).

Know where you-r kid is in his moral development. At one stage, you will concretely input moral ideas that he sees as absolute truth. Later in his development, you will engage with him as an active participant in his moral development, much like you might debate with a friend about a controversial issue (with simpler language).

Age: 5 to 9 years old

Type: Heteronomous (moral realism)

Belief: Children see morality through the eyes of others, such as parents, teachers, and the law. They accept that breaking these rules leads to punishment. Rules are absolute and unchanging.

Role of parent: The parent's job is to be clear and intentional with the moral values they want to establish in their children. These values are seen as absolute.

Age: 9 to 10 years old

Type: Autonomous morality (moral relativism)

Belief: Children base morality on their own rules. Morality is based on intentions and consequences. Because these kids have moved away from egocentricism (as described earlier), they can see the variation in morality across people. Morality is not rigid but flexible and changing based on who is looking. This view carries through to adulthood. For example, one person might see stealing as completely immoral no matter what, while another might see the intention or need for stealing (i.e., poverty) as a determinant of whether or not something is immoral.

Role of parent: The parent's role is to engage with children as an active participant in building their own morality. Ask questions about moral decision making, debate, offer your perspective, and know that your son will ultimately see morality through his own lens. You still have an impact on his beliefs but your view is not absolute in his eyes anymore.

This theory was fundamental to my own growth as a parent because it pushed me to speak with my boys about gender, consent, empathy, and sexual development sooner rather than later. Before I understood this theory, I would have assumed this content was too mature and that my boys were not developed enough to engage in a conversation. I was wrong.

Around age five, there is very little association or meaning for boys when talking about sex, consent, and relationships. You actually have a very captive audience in terms of moral development. You can consciously input values that hold true for you and your family. It is actually a breath of fresh air to speak with someone who isn't buried in meaning around sexuality. For your boy, it's just nuts and bolts. If you embrace the conversation, it can be fun, connecting, and potentially reparative for those of us who experienced a lot of shame and awkwardness around these conversations (if you even had them) growing up. Practice diving in headfirst. I promise, you won't regret it.

Our boys will develop their own beliefs as they age, but offering an axiom to work from will help keep them and others safe in the future. If our sons can fundamentally know that touching people when they don't want to be touched is wrong, then those beliefs act as a grounding force as they move forward in their moral development. Yes, this belief might morph into something else, but as parents we have done our part in consciously building a moral blueprint for them. The scripts written into our boys' brains from childhood shape who they become as people and partners.[44]

Healthy, Normal Sexual Behavior

Now you have some references to come back to when you are trying to understand your developing boy. So how can we know when sexual behaviors and conversations are normal and when they indicate a problem? Remember that these conversations are not just about physical development but also about beliefs, relationships, identity, and empathy for others.

The tables below are adapted from the National Child Traumatic Stress Network and help parents get a sense of normative sexual development, what kids might say and do, and how parents can respond. Much of what freaks parents out (for example, when my preschool daughter used to hump everything) is often very typical and reflects healthy development.

Signs of Normal Sexual Behavior in Children Under 12[45]

Parents worry when they catch their son "playing doctor" with a friend or touching his penis, but most of this behavior is normal. Boys don't just all of a sudden hit puberty and become interested in sex—sexual development starts in utero and slowly evolves throughout childhood. If (or when) you find your son engaged in sexual behavior with another child and are trying to figure out if it is normal, consider these things:

- It happens between children that know each other and have an ongoing, mutual friendship.

- There is mutuality in the relationship—similar age and emotional, physical, and cognitive development.

- It is infrequent.

- It is considered fun and playful (not upsetting).

- Kids are redirectable when "caught."

Signs that the Sexual Behavior Is Less Typical and Needs Exploration[46]

Not all sexual behavior is normal, though. Playing doctor in a reciprocal relationship is normal, but pain, power differentials between kids, and distress is not. Ask yourself, *Is this a balanced, "fun" exploration experience for all involved, or does it seem unbalanced, distressing, and uncomfortable for one or more of the children?* Follow your gut here and ask questions.

- The behavior is beyond the child's developmental stage (for example, intercourse or insertion of objects rather than touching).

- The child is distressed.

- The behavior interferes with the child's functioning on some level: emotional, physical, academic, or social.

- It involves coercion, pressure, or aggression.

- The behavior does not redirect easily by adults.

If you are concerned, talk with your son about his feelings and the situation, and consult with your pediatrician.

For an easy overview of typical behaviors that arise during different stages and suggestions for how to respond, please take a look at the Sex Talk with Kids Cheat Sheet found at the back of this book.

Behavior in Kids Ages 0 to 6

During this age, it is completely normal for boys (and girls) to become curious about their bodies and others' bodies too. Touching their genitals, using potty talk, and mimicking sexual behavior (like kissing) is well within expected development.

The moniker "Captain Poopy Pants" would often be hurled between my kids. It always landed as something funny and as an insult, both of which reinforced the behavior (potty talk). A behavior is controlled by its consequences.[47] To extinguish a behavior, the best approach is to ignore the "bad behavior" and positively reinforce the "good" ones. Ignore the potty talk and reinforce through praise or by rewarding your child with something meaningful when he is sitting nicely at the dinner table and using appropriate language.

Have you ever walked into your young son's room and seen him naked on his bed and his friend inspecting his erect penis? If so, it's likely you froze in horror and didn't know what to do or say. Despite this being totally horrifying and unexpected to many parents, "playing doctor" is completely normal for kids this age. Our job is to set limits, note the curiosity, and not completely freak out. Yes, it is okay to let the child know what is okay and what isn't, and being thoughtful about what message is conveyed is also important, so as to not shame the child around normal curiosity.

Try this: "Time to get dressed boys. I see you are curious about each other's bodies, and that is completely normal, but we don't touch or look at each other's penises." Parents can also let their kids know that when they are playing in their rooms the door has to be kept open. It's also good practice to let the other child's parents know what happened so that they aren't shocked later on if their child says anything. See it as an opportunity to help normalize these conversations about developmentally appropriate sexual behaviors and find ways to set boundaries that work for your family.

Kids' sexual development begins in utero, but there is a cultural misnomer that sexual development doesn't start until puberty. Parents are often embarrassed when their child says something "inappropriate" or grabs his mother's breast, but this is all part of their learning. Yes, it is the parent's job to help the child socialize and set limits, but the shame, embarrassment, and sometimes guilt parents feel is completely unnecessary and can actually interfere with development.

If a boy senses uncomfortable emotions from a parent, he internalizes the feeling that these behaviors are abnormal and not tolerated. This can lead to boys who turn into men who aren't comfortable with their sexuality or those of others, and don't know how to process their feelings and sexual desires. Therefore, it is important to remember that this type of curiosity is natural, and that we need to choose how we respond very carefully. We do not want to create any shameful, negative associations. The best way to approach this is as an observer while managing your own internal reactions and emotions.

In an ideal world, you would have started talking to your son before age six about sex, bodies, and relationships, but my hunch is that you might not be buying this book when you have a six-month-old son. Don't fret if you have either intentionally or unintentionally had your head in the sand for the past few years. It is never too late to start talking with your son. Stay ahead of the game and don't wait for him to approach you. Buy a book about bodies and have it on hand. Give it to him but don't force it. Know sex and body questions are coming, if they haven't already, so have the book available for when those questions arise. For some great books, check out the Suggested Reading List at this book's website, http://www.newharbinger.com/46677.

Behavior in Kids Ages 6 to 12

At this age, kids are in the social world. We might still think of them as our little babies, but they are learning a lot! Even if you strictly regulate media use, your son's friends don't have the same rules. Expect that they are visiting YouTube and other sites where they will stumble across "adult material." You do not need to deep dive into explaining pornography yet (although for some kids, they might be ready to hear what it is), but talk with your boy about what he might see—nude people, bad words, adults doing adult things, and so on. Research found that the average age of youth exposure to pornography is eleven.[48] You must also speak with him about how to keep himself and his information safe from online strangers. Be candid. Honest. Concrete. And not alarmist.

The questions I've fielded from my eight- to ten-year-old boys in the past year include: What is sex? What is an STD and how do you get one? What is a pimp? How do gay women have babies? Why does my penis stick up sometimes? Many of these were prompted by things they learned from friends or online. If you have not yet fielded these types of questions, know they are just around the corner or already on his mind—and are totally normal.

My son said, "You fingered me!" in reference to me accidentally showing my middle finger as I reached for something. I very calmly said, "Fingering is actually when you put your finger in someone's vagina. You mean I just showed you my middle finger." He said okay and moved on.

The best approach is to stay as cool as you can. With time, you will see that when you don't get awkward, your son doesn't get awkward. If you are caught off guard (which is almost always), memorize this: "That is a great question. Let me think about it for a second. What makes you ask and what have you heard?" Get him talking and collect a bit of information about what he knows to help you guide the response. Know that you are stepping into a dialogue and that it isn't your job to have all the answers. Your job is to join a conversation with your son, and if there are things you don't know (like "What is it called when people don't really have a whole penis or a vagina?"; it's "intersex," for the record), that is okay. Don't fake it. Help him get the answers somewhere else, together. One of the most important things here is that you send the message that you are comfortable talking about sex—you will help him find the answers, and no topic is off-limits. Expect that you will not know all the answers.

Behavior in Kids Ages 11 to 18

Parents always say, "Kids grow up so fast." And that is true. It feels like one day you are talking about video games, and the next it is about who hooked up with who (if you are lucky enough to be included in the conversation). This is when the conversations all of a sudden change from feeling pediatric to beyond parents' pay grade, and quite often parents are unprepared and do not know how to respond to mature conversations.

But if you have done the front-end work of establishing a strong relationship and open dialogue about talking about sex, this stage is so much easier. Navigating social dynamics, sexual and relational safety, and healthy lifestyle choices all come crashing to the forefront of parenting at this stage.

A twenty-year-old patient once shared, "I remember watching porno with some friends when I was twelve. It was exciting and interesting, and we were all into it. We would sit in a group and watch and touch ourselves. For a while, we did it almost every day after school. At the time, it seemed totally normal and not creepy—a new thing to explore that was awesome. When I got older and looked back, I felt weird about it. Ashamed for some reason." Sexual exploration with others is also normative, although men often look back at these experiences and feel shame around them or as if they did something wrong.

As kids grow up and learn more about the very strong and clear homophobic messaging in our culture, boys look back at normative earlier experiences with shame, judgment, and a lot of questions about themselves. So, hear me parents and people out there: you aren't necessarily gay because you touched yourselves with friends. You might be, and that is totally cool, but either way this behavior is a normal part of the process for many boys.

Regardless of our moral beliefs, 57 percent of teens seek out porn at least monthly, so it is worth talking about.[49] The strongest predictor of porn use is being male.[50] There are many mixed messages and strong feelings about pornography due to its reputation of subordinating and hurting women,[51] even though 30 percent of porn users are female.[52] Oftentimes, parents look to their own viewing histories and feel like watching porn is not a big deal, while at the same time worry that their son is going to be a violent rapist or sex addict—or, at the very least, have skewed sexual expectations—if he watches porn. The former is less likely than the latter.

I recently heard a debate among relationship and sex therapists about whether porn consumption is healthy.[53] The takeaway was that all porn is not created equal. Porn is a tool, and it is how we use it that makes it problematic or not. Is it a disservice to other parts of our life? Are we avoiding or neglecting real-life relationships? Is it managing anxiety or other mental health issues? Is it creating unrealistic sexual standards or helping us better understand our own fantasies and sexual worlds? A gang rape video is not the same as watching a sexual encounter that is more balanced in power. And for gay boys, pornography might be the only access to watch gay relationships between men and help build their erotic inner worlds, acting to educate and liberate an otherwise closeted group of people.[54]

The goal is to not become the Internet police or live-in porn monitor but rather talk about what is out there—the variety, the positive, the negative, and how your son feels about it. Ask candid questions about how he feels before, during, and after he watches so he gains more awareness about how it affects him. Encourage this self-awareness by prompting him to contemplate—internally and not necessarily out loud with you—what porn he likes. Why? What does he get out of it? Share how it can inform how he sees romantic partners and hopes for his own sexual life. What function does it play for him? Does it help create his fantasy life or hinder reality? This can help your son assess whether it is something he wants in his life and teach him to make better decisions for himself.

Like all other types of conversations, take a curious approach around how porn is impacting your son rather than the likely authoritarian, punitive approach you know from growing up. Create space for him to ask questions and share. The impact of a *Playboy* stuffed in the corner of the garage is different than virtual-reality-type online sexual experiences available twenty-four hours a day for our young boys since the advent of the World Wide Web.[55] It's best to be honest about that.

Aside from porn, at this point, there is much less talk about the mechanics of sex and more about teaching about things like consent, healthy relationships, safe sex, boundaries, exploring one's own comfort, safe exploration, body shame and power, empathy, and knowing how to talk about sexual issues with others. Many teens and young adults are ill-informed about developing loving and lasting intimate relationships and are anxious about developing them.

Making Caring Common (https://mcc.gse.harvard.edu) is a wonderful resource for parents and boys on how to develop lasting, intimate, and safe romantic relationships. Its survey of three thousand high schoolers and young adults found that 70 percent of young adults wished they had received more information on the emotional aspects of a romantic relationship.[56] And among other beliefs you probably don't realize your kid has, the survey found that 32 percent of males and 22 percent of females think men should be dominant in romantic relationships.

Most of the respondents had never spoken with their parents about key aspects of safe, healthy, reciprocal relationships. With parents' awkwardness around the topic of sex, it's not surprising that 58 percent of respondents had never had a conversation with their parents about the importance of "being a caring and respectful sexual partner." Yet a large majority of respondents who had engaged in these conversations with parents described them as at least somewhat influential.

Take a cue from Making Caring Common and be sure to talk to your son about these essential topics:

- Being sure his partner wants to have sex and is comfortable doing so before having sex

- Assuring his own comfort level before engaging in sex

- The importance of not pressuring someone to have sex with him

- The importance of not continuing to ask someone to have sex after they have said no

- The importance of not having sex with someone who is too intoxicated or impaired to make a decision about sex

At this stage, think of yourself as the question-asker who holds the options up in front of your teen and helps him think through the long-term consequences of his actions. Of course, you have family values and certain rules of the house, and your job is to help your teenager make sound decisions as he lives within those boundaries.

You might say something like: "So, you want to have sex with Madison? Imagine you get to the party tonight and you get the sense she wants to make out with you. What are all of your options? What is the upside and downside of each? How do you expect to feel in each of them? How would you feel in the moment and tomorrow? How do you think she might feel in the moment and tomorrow? What would or wouldn't affect your decision making? Her decision making? You are a smart, kind boy, and all your answers live within you. I am here to help sort them alongside you. Let's honestly look at all the options." For more examples of ways to respond, feel free to take a look at the Sex Talk with Kids Cheat Sheet guide at the back of this book.

Feminist Takeaways

While there's clearly a lot to consider here, my hope is that by sharing some theoretical underpinnings and translating them to everyday parenting, you will feel better prepared for these conversations. You don't need to know all of this at once, but come back to the pieces you find relevant when you are in a particular stage with your son.

I don't share all of this with you to induce fear. Instead, I want to normalize it. You cannot change his biological course (he *will* grow from a fumbling little baby to a sexualized man), but you can change the accompanying narrative around how your boy sees himself and others today and in the future. Proper self-reflection, self-awareness, accountability, empathy, connection, and learning to self-correct: this is how he will build a solid internal compass that will last a lifetime. Help him get there.

Ultimately, trust yourself. You know your son the best. Educate yourself, educate your son, acknowledge the process, and allow your boy to make his own mistakes with you by his side. Use your intuitive knowledge and common sense, and let these frameworks guide you when you need a hand.

CHAPTER 3

Build Inner Resources to Raise Allies

Feminism is about equality for everyone. If you want to raise a feminist boy who believes in equality and will work to include women's needs and wants into the system in which we live, then he must be an *ally*. An ally is someone in a dominant group who works to end oppression in a marginalized group.[57] In this case, we are focused on raising boys (the dominant group) who will work to end oppression for women and all genders, although the approach we are using can help raise boys who are allies to everyone.

Most of the messaging in our culture around what is valued and good for everyone is focused on men and "masculine" traits such as strength, emotional disconnection, independence, and competitiveness.[58] Let's pause for a minute and realize that in everyday language we often default to saying "he" instead of "she" or "they." We say "policeman" instead of "police," "mankind" instead of "humankind." These are everyday ways in which sexism comes up.

Who is most often in control? Look around at work. Who is in charge of our country? It's easy to see we have created a society that values masculinity and men over femininity and women. The blueprint for everything is based on men and their needs, which is what we call the *patriarchy*. This discussion is not just about being equal, it is about having women's voices and needs built into the blueprint too.

Privilege isn't one dimensional or linear, though. Privilege is clearly intersectional: a poor, disabled white man's power is less socially valued than a wealthy, athletic white man's power. A poor Black man is commonly viewed as a threat—regardless of the good he does in society. Add sexual preference, gender, age, and how well looks match ideal images of beauty, and you can see how power and privilege, and disadvantage and discrimination, are simultaneously overlapping and interdependent. It creates a complicated hierarchy of whose voice matters most in society.

Wherever in the intersectional hierarchy our sons stand, they share high societal ranking as boys. Among all people, my two sons are very privileged because of their nationality (American), skin color (white), class (upper-middle), sex (male), religion (Christian), and language (English and French). Having this status does not mean that they don't feel pain or have their own worries. It means they have opportunities offered to them by just being born who they are because the established system—the patriarchy—is built to support them.

Jump forward to high school and college, and it's no wonder the rates of rape are one in five for women, with more than 90 percent of the assailants being male, according to a 2010 survey on sexual violence in the US.[59] Our boys' values shape the choices they make. If they feel entitled to take what they want because they have learned it's their right to get it, of course rates of sexual assault will continue to be high.

As parents, it is our job to help them understand how their societal positioning buffers life struggles and actively boosts them at all levels. Rather than using their position to seek advantage over others; coast into high-paying, decision-making leadership roles; or even cause harm in the process of getting what they want, they can step outside themselves. They can be part of more inclusive and balanced environments—whether at school, with friends, or when establishing groups—with the goal of creating an inclusive culture.

Boys of all ages can be allies. Think of the little guy who gives a hug to anyone in tears. Or who invites his female preschool classmate to join him in the sandbox to play with trucks. Or who sits with the transgender girl at the lunch table because they both like the cartoon *Steven Universe*. Or who's likeability influences other kids to join him to protest for gender-neutral bathrooms. Or who encounters the truth of his Asian girlfriend's experience and accepts that his view was too narrow and even wrong. All of these boys are feminists and allies because they believe in equality, perceive that they always need to be learning from others, and are aware that social systems must change to better support all people.

For my sons, budding allyship was when my then-nine-year-old told his friends to "cut it out" when they were teasing a classmate for having a girlfriend. Or when my six-year-old articulated that a victim of murder by a police officer was killed because of racism. Or when my eleven-year-old held his friend's private secret in confidence. Being an ally is not just about acceptance, it is about being trustworthy and available to emotionally support others.

Family allyship is when you participate as a group in a small or large cause—walking in the Women's March, speaking up against the homophobic-tinted humor that might arise at a family holiday, or listening to a family friend share a painful story of persecution. Allyship in families is about self-awareness, personal and familial accountability, speaking up, and creating a safe and inclusive space for everyone to share all of themselves without fear of judgment.

The question many parents ask is, "Can I teach my son to be an ally, or is he just born with empathy?" People wonder if an ally is just an empathic person. The two are overlapping but different. They overlap in the sense that allies are *empathic*; that is, they understand what another person might feel in a situation. For example, an empath might feel an internal sadness when he sees the kid in the wheelchair being left out of the playground game. But the two roles are different in that being empathic is not enough to be an ally; an ally acts on the feeling and does something to make the environment more inclusive and accepting of everybody. Empathy is understanding the feelings of another; allyship is understanding the feelings of another and doing something to make the environment more inclusive. An ally not only gets what the kid in the wheelchair might feel, he asks the kid if he wants to play and what the best way for him to play is.

The good news is that all of this is teachable. As we help build stronger, more centered, emotionally durable boys, we also help change the culture in which we live. The current model of raising boys makes it clear that emotions need to be suppressed, being "hard" and "strong" is crucial, and anything that is perceived as feminine is anti-male. The new feminist model is the opposite. Emotions are welcomed and developing emotional intelligence is of utmost importance. With that comes an awareness and acceptance of all emotions, and showing them is a sign of strength. And last, all types of gender expression are welcome. Boys come in all shapes, sizes, and colors. Being feminine or masculine or somewhere in between share at least one commonality: a type of boy.

One criticism of raising feminist boys is that "boys are boys" and should be celebrated as such, not raised feminine. This is a misnomer. Feminist boys aren't necessarily *feminine* boys—although they can be. A feminist boy is simply a boy who believes in equality and access for all. A feminist boy is emotionally tuned in, self-aware, and takes action to create an equitable environment.

The way you raise your son is closely tied to his ability to create inclusive environments and genuinely appreciate and support all people. Let's dive deeper and think through what this actually looks like and how you can achieve this at home. Let's make the idea of parenting for feminism more concrete.

Cultivating Healthy Attunement and Attachment

Attunement (responsiveness to your child) creates *attachment* (a connection). This connection is critically important in helping people develop self-esteem and healthier relationships across their lifespan.

Boys with secure attachments are better allies because they have the internal resources to look beyond themselves. With a secure base and healthy self-esteem, they are able to develop compassion and empathy for others. Later in this chapter, I'll share ways to encourage the development of key aspects required to be an ally: knowledge and skills, openness and support, and oppression awareness.[60] First, here are ways to lay the foundation so your son can stand for equality.

Attunement

So, what is attunement? Dr. Dan Siegel said, "Attunement is the reactiveness we have to another person. It is the process by which we form relationships."[61] Think of a time when you were truly heard, felt, and seen by someone. The person connected with your inner state and was able to step outside of their own needs and wants in that moment. That is attunement.

When you attune to your son's needs, he connects with his emotional state and yours on a deep level—this builds the emotional framework from which he will live his life.

Attunement in babies looks like an infant crying, a caregiver noticing, and responding to the baby's needs. Consistent response to a baby's needs creates a secure attachment, which is a happy baby who trusts that he will be responded to and cared for. This crying baby looks for his primary caregiver, clings to them when they respond to his needs, and settles down with some ease. The baby feels secure in his parent's arms since his parent responded to him effectively, meeting his needs in a reasonable amount of time. This is attunement.

Older boys are physically bigger and emotionally more developed but not hugely different in other ways. Attunement looks like a parent being able to effectively read their son. My nine-year-old came home from school and said that everything "is fine," but I saw in his face and from his nonverbal cues that something was wrong. I went to his room and sat with him, knowing he would open up and share if I stuck around long enough. After sitting on his bed for twenty minutes, he shared that another kid made fun of his new haircut. He was embarrassed and doubted that his new mohawk was a good choice. That is attunement in older kids. An attuned kid is more likely to be kind, empathic, and loving to others since he has learned that "the world is generally safe" in his relationship with his parents, and he feels loved.

Parents who are attuned to their son's needs create an environment where he can successfully attach to them. Secure attachments to early caregivers provide a safe base from which children are free to explore and connect with others because they trust relationships and people.

Attunement isn't just noticing and empathizing with your son's feelings in the moment, it is caring at its deepest level—knowing what is important to him, noticing it, and naming it. If a young boy loves football, he'll know all the teams, player statistics, and all the plays. When you begin a conversation by asking about the latest professional football game he went to, and even name his favorite player, his face will light up. He will be moved by the fact that you remembered and know him so well, and he'll readily open up to you in the conversation. That is an example of attunement.

You can attune to your son at any age. Although the way you attune might change with your son's development, there are some basics that remain consistent across time and space.

- **Pay attention to your nonverbal communication.** Much of what we communicate is nonverbal. Maintain eye contact, put your phone down when your son is talking, and let him know that what he is sharing is important to you.

- **Follow your child's lead.** Sometimes your son wants to talk and other times he does not. Sometimes he wants to be close and other times he does not. Notice and name what you see ("I sense you don't feel like talking now. Is that right?") and let him know you respect his needs ("That is okay. I need space at times too. I am here when you feel ready").

- **Empathize and validate his emotions.** Whenever your son shares an emotion, reflect the emotion back ("It sounds like you were really sad then") and validate his feelings ("I can see how you would feel that way").

- **Be curious about his experience.** Park the advice-giving. Ask open-ended questions like, "How was soccer for you today?" "What was an upside and downside of the party last night?" "If you had a magic wand, what would you change about your classroom or teachers?" Be cautious to not give ideas about how to handle situations, but ask deepening questions like, "I can see how you would feel that way. If you had to do it again, what would you do differently?" Ask questions that get to the thoughts and feelings under the level of where he is currently at. Imagine digging lower and lower to get to the truest, deepest core feeling and thought. Ask yourself, *What is the thought under that thought?* Ask your son that too. People feel seen, heard, and attuned to when you understand their core human experience. Dig for it.

Attachment

Attunement and attachment often go together but are a bit different. Attachment is a close emotional bond between two people and generally refers to the connection between a child and their parent (or early caregiver).[62] Attachment usually forms in healthy relationships when people attune to each other's needs. Children attach to responsive caregivers and, at a very fundamental level, learn that people are loving and that the world is safe. This allows them to move from the relationship with the primary caregiver to relationships with other people. Although attachment styles are thought to be set within the first year and a half of a baby's life, these relational patterns last a lifetime—although they can change with awareness and work.[63]

Understanding types of attachment helps you not only have a framework to understand your son's healthiest development, it names the unspoken dynamic that you might feel but not understand. For example, I was recently working with Chris, who was dating Tina, who has a nine-year-old son, Eric. Tina had lost her husband to cancer when Eric was three years old. When Tina and Chris began dating, everything seemed wonderful. Eric took to Chris very well. Tina was thrilled because Eric had "ruined" many of her past relationships by driving her boyfriends away—acting out, being mean, and having tantrums when men would visit. Chris and Eric spent a lot of time together—going to baseball games, hanging out together, and just generally connecting. Early on, Chris had Eric over for boys' weekend sleepovers, and Eric suggested he wanted Chris to marry his mother.

After some time and as the relationships grew closer, Eric began acting out and pushing boundaries. He was disrespectful and argumentative. In our work, it became clear that Eric has an anxious attachment style. Intimacy and closeness are tied with vulnerability and loss for this little boy who had already endured so much. He desperately wanted a father figure but feared the loss of closeness, which he had learned inevitably comes (through the loss of his own father and then subsequent relationships his mother would have). Understanding this helped Chris understand Eric and talk with him about his underlying fear. Rather than responding to the (obnoxious!)

behavior, both Tina and Chris could empathize with Eric's fear and help change the course of the relationship for them all.

Now let's look at four the different types of attachment.

Disorganized Attachment Style

A boy with a disorganized attachment style is one who has mixed feelings toward his parents due to unpredictable behavior on the caregiver's part. When a parent leaves and returns, these children run up to the parent upon return but then pull away, hit them, or curl up on the floor and show confused behavior. This is because all babies are wired to seek comfort from adults, particularly their caregivers, as their survival depends on it.

When a parent is abusive (emotionally, physically, or sexually), they become the source of pain and trauma and comfort at the same time, which deprives the child of a safe, workable way to get his needs met. Unfortunately, these kids are the ones with the worst long-term outcomes. They don't have healthy ways to self-soothe, don't trust people, have difficulty in social connection and interaction, and don't manage stress well. All of these factors compound as life goes on because their behavior can be aggressive or hostile, as they have fundamentally learned the world is unsafe and people aren't to be trusted.

If you see relationally disorganized behavior in your son (which is not the same as being a disorganized kid who forgets his homework and leaves his socks lying around), ask yourself if your son has a history of unpredictability or lack of safety in an important relationship in his life. Are you potentially making him feel unsafe or that your ability to take care of him is compromised in some way? Did someone else make him, or is currently making him, feel this way? Does he perceive you as threatening or unpredictable? How can you build safety and security into your relationship with him?

Boys with this type of attachment often have well-intentioned and loving parents who struggle with healthy caretaking due to other issues like mental health problems, substance abuse problems, or lack of knowledge around healthy relationships and parenting.

If you think your son might have a disorganized attachment style, you should focus on building safety, security, and predictability into the relationship. You and your child would benefit from seeking help from a mental health professional. Attachment styles can change, but it takes focus and work.

Avoidant Attachment Style

An avoidant boy is one who ends up shutting down his needs as a response to an unemotional or unresponsive primary caregiver. Even when parents leave a room and return, children with avoidant attachment will resist being close to their caregivers, although they had a need and want for closeness and sought it by just being in close physical proximity. Imagine the toddler who cries when he is hungry and nobody responds. Eventually, he will find a way to get a snack himself—and avoid crying all together.

These boys are often very self-reliant, but it comes from a place of need, and this independence develops prematurely in lieu of close connection. They are good at self-soothing and taking care of themselves, but their world becomes insular—they don't feel they need others and miss out on intimacy. These qualities fit well within our cultural framework of masculinity, where we expect boys to be emotionless and suppress their emotional needs and wants.

Avoidant behavior in your son, not to be confused with a kid who avoids homework or chores, will show up as avoiding close emotional relationships. Ask yourself if he had an unresponsive early caregiver. Are you potentially unresponsive in some ways? This can be as extreme as emotional neglect and as nuanced as a parent who is chronically "too busy" with work and does not take interest in their son's emotional life and lived experience. It can also be the parent with a drinking problem or another issue that gets in the way of being an emotionally connected parent.

If you think your son might have an avoidant attachment style, find a way to demonstrate your interest, love, and reliability. Remember, avoidant boys are the independent ones who have learned others can't be counted on, so they must take care of themselves. Show your son that you can be counted on. If you say something like, "I will be at your game today," then make sure you are at the game.

Changing an avoidance attachment is not just about showing up physically but, more important, showing up emotionally. Show your interest in his emotional life. Ask open-ended and emotionally focused questions, as described earlier. Show him that there is room for his thoughts, feelings, and experiences in the relationship with you—that you love and care for him, and want to know what makes him tick.

Anxious Attachment Style

A child who has an anxious attachment is one who feels anxious about separating from his parent because the parent's behavior and responsiveness is unpredictable.[64] The parent can infantilize the boy, stifling his autonomy and willingness to separate and explore. As older kids and adults, these are people who can be clingy, hard to pacify, and immature. When people have this attachment style, their inner world and the world with the people closest to them feels uncertain, so there is little room to be empathic and extend out in their circle of concern.

If you think your son might have an anxious attachment style, ask yourself if you or someone else has sent the message to your son that you must control everything and that the world is unsafe without you (or another caregiver). Have you unconsciously created a situation where you have shown your love and care through protecting and doing everything for your son, so much that he has not had the opportunity to explore and build his own set of skills outside of you? Are you overly involved and protective? Although this parenting style is often well intentioned, it is detrimental to healthy emotional attachment.

If this resonates with you, you are probably a parent who needs to back off a little. Continue with lots of love but pull back on the "doing for" tasks. Work on your own ability to separate from your son. What needs are you meeting through being overly interventionist and controlling? Do you trust that your son can safely explore, fumble, fall, get up, learn, and grow? If not, why not? Is that a *you* thing or a *him* thing, meaning is it old baggage from *your* childhood that you are bringing to the parenting relationship, or is it a true concern today (for example, you have a son with special needs who needs much of your attention and control)?

Regardless of who your son is and what his needs are, how can you find ways (given his unique needs) for him to explore and have more control in his own life? Can your little one play in the yard alone without you? Can your big boy bike across town to the market? Can your high schooler go out for the night without you tracking or calling him every hour?

Find ways to back off and trust your son more. It is in the moments of freedom and independence when he will learn more about himself, build self-efficacy, and learn how to fail and recover.

Secure Attachment Style

A securely attached boy is one who expresses his emotion when a caregiver leaves but can settle himself down and respond affectionately when they return. As this boy gets older, this style remains the same. He can be open in relationships, understand others, express his emotion, self-soothe, and tolerate frustration. He is the teenager who falls madly in love with his first true love, is open and emotional with them, and is devastated when they break up—but he can move on with time and in due process.

He has healthy emotional relationships in which can he attach appropriately, express sadness at unwanted endings, and has the self-esteem to trust he will be okay. These guys empathize more and understand others effectively, because they are fundamentally more connected with themselves and the emotional experience of trusting relationships. These boys are best primed to be good allies, although there are a number of other factors that contribute to being a good ally as well.

If you think your son has a secure attachment, bravo! You have found the balance between secure love and attention, and trust and freedom to explore. Keep focusing on a warm, emotionally focused, reciprocal relationship with your son that has both clear boundaries and expectations, plus lots of room for him to explore and learn. Although your son will change over time, his need for love, security, and space to explore remains consistent.

To help your son form a secure attachment, the ultimate goal is to foster a connected relationship. To achieve that, maintain connection during times of both ease and frustration and difficulty. You can address troubling behavior and maintain a connected relationship. Never use your love, or withdrawal of love, as a punishment. Boys who feel understood and loved are free to understand and love others.

As a psychologist who sees many families in my practice, it's clear that loved, securely attached kids are the ones most likely to help others, since they have capacity for awareness of self and other, empathy, and stronger connection. This chapter is filled with ways to raise emotionally healthy sons for their benefit, your benefit, and as a social change agent. This is the power you have in your hand, right now, as you shape the next generation of men.

Healthy Emotional Development

Healthy emotional development is the ability to understand who you are, notice and understand what you are feeling and why, express these feelings effectively with others, and sustain positive relationships with people. This is also called *emotional intelligence* (EI). People with high EI generally feel better and are better allies and friends to others. They have enough emotional gas in their tank to go the distance for someone else and therefore are best primed to be feminist boys. Harvard found that close relationships, made possible by higher emotional intelligence, predict lifelong happiness and health.[65]

An example of someone with high emotional intelligence is a partner who always remembers your special days, is available to you when you feel down, and finds a way to balance being present and giving enough space. They send notes on anniversaries and take the extra minute to stop and get flowers every once in a while—just because they know you love tulips. Or picks up your favorite Thai food, although it is twenty minutes off the path. We all know these people—they are comfortable and confident enough to share themselves freely and with appropriate awareness of others. They are flexible, resilient, creative, empathic, and generally good listeners. They also often have high self-esteem. People feel seen, heard, and appreciated with these types of people.[66]

Boys with high EI are better at self-soothing when upset and can calm themselves on a physiological level (lower their heart rates) and therefore have the benefit of better physical health too.[67] They have more friends and understand people better. Children with high emotional intelligence empathize with their peers, name emotions, and have good self-regulation even when frustrated or upset. Peers and adults tend to like them because they are tuned in to the emotional tone of the environment. He is the boy in class who takes turns, helps others, and is flexible with change, although he might feel disappointed.

What does low EI look like? Here's an example. A successful, incredibly smart, high-achieving student, who has the best intentions and who can be kind and caring, informally invites an entire class to an end-of-the-year celebration at his home. He later decides it makes more sense to gather a limited group and doesn't think to tell the rest of the class that they are no longer invited. His friend eventually spreads the news when people ask what date to save. He doesn't notice that there are big feelings brewing below the surface for many—from those who are going and for those who aren't. He even minimizes it when a friend raises it as a potential issue. All this is made worse by the fact that the party ended up being almost exclusively male. This is low emotional intelligence, an inability to consider the feelings of others.

People with low EI get stressed easily and either don't assert themselves enough or do it too aggressively and without appropriate regard for others. They hold grudges, have poor emotional coping, focus on others' mistakes, and don't know their own emotional triggers. People around them often feel that they don't know what to expect and walk around on eggshells. Sadly, people with low emotional intelligence often have poor self-esteem underneath the frustrating outer shell.[68]

Low EI kids are the ones who often frustrate their peers, might have behavioral issues in school, have poor emotional coping, and often seem to think the world revolves around them. It is the kid who doesn't notice peers reacting negatively, pushes others when he is frustrated, and has regular meltdowns when things don't go his way. It can also be the kid who is quiet but then blows up when angered, or the cranky kid who has poor frustration tolerance and pulls away from social situations because he cannot read the room. Low emotional intelligence comes in different forms, but the long and short of it is that he is not tuned in to the feelings and reactions of others, and doesn't have effective communication skills to negotiate emotional situations. He hasn't learned effective skills from the adults around him.

The Five Elements of Emotional Intelligence

Daniel Goleman's seminal book, *Emotional Intelligence: Why It Can Matter More Than IQ*, identifies five important elements of EI: self-awareness, self-regulation, motivation, empathy, and social skills. Unlike one's intelligence quotient (IQ), EI skills can be developed and improved upon, although it is often easier the younger one practices.

Self-awareness refers to self-focused attention or knowledge,[69] meaning the ability to recognize one's own emotions and how they impact others. Self-aware boys link how their emotions and behaviors affect others. For example, boys are often caught between saying something they know is hurtful (like a sexist joke) and the pressure to be masculine. Self-aware boys have the insight to notice how these comments often offend their peers. Self-awareness is the first step in *self-reflection*, which helps us notice and understand what we want to change within ourselves. Self-reflective boys will explore the pull between what they are trying to achieve socially and the hurt they cause in others. These guys wrestle with how to meet their goals and change their behaviors, like what they say, to inflict less harm and become kinder.

Self-regulation is the control of one's behavior through monitoring and reflection,[70] which helps people manage their difficult emotions and be flexible to change. Once a boy has the ability to notice his own emotions and reflect on their impact, he can then choose how he responds. That is self-regulation. These are the boys who walk away from a fight rather than pummel their opponent on the soccer field.

Motivation is the impetus that drives our behavior in search of internal (or external) gratification.[71] Boys who are motivated are the ones who get things done to feel accomplished and successful. These are the kids who work hard, whether in school, sports, art, or music.

Empathy is understanding someone's emotional experience from their frame of reference, rather than from one's own.[72] Empathy is not the same as compassion. It is being able to separate from one's own feelings in order to perceive what someone else feels. These are the boys who care strongly for others' emotions, because they can feel what it is like to be them.

Social skills are a learned set of abilities that allow a person to behave appropriately in a social context.[73] In the United States, the most valued skills are assertiveness, emotional flexibility, effective communication, ability to connect with people, interpersonal problem solving, and the ability to manage one's feelings, thoughts, and behaviors. Boys with strong social skills are the ones who are generally accepted by peers and adults, can be flexible so their behavior fits the context, and gain approval from others.

There are some biological predispositions, like temperament and capacity for social skills, that shapes a boy's ability to develop strong emotional intelligence,[74] but unlike intellectual intelligence, EI can grow with attention and practice. But before skills can be practiced, a solid sense of self-esteem has to be established. Remember, self-esteem and emotional intelligence are related. Parents can help build self-esteem through attunement and attachment, and the earlier parents pay attention to this, the easier the work will be.

Cultivating EI in Your Son

The ability to empathize with and read others is fundamental in feminism. To promote equality for everyone, you must be willing and able to understand how it feels to be someone else. The good news is that this can be learned. Here are ways to cultivate emotional intelligence in your son.

- **Model emotional intelligence.** Do this in your words and behaviors. Talk about your feelings (all of them) and show that you value emotional communication.

- **Demonstrate unconditional love.** There is nothing your son can do to make you love him less. His behavior is not linked to your love.

- **Show authenticity.** Being attuned and attached doesn't mean you have to always agree; it means you can validate your boy's emotional experience while being yourself completely. When you are in disagreement or disapproval, it's okay to both name your son's emotional experience and your reaction (apart from his experience). For example, your seven-year-old son might say, "All I want is a pocketknife." And you might respond authentically, "I can see how a pocket-knife seems so cool. You could cut sticks and it would be fun to make etchings. There is a part of me that cringes even thinking about that, though. The fact that the knife might slip and seriously slice your finger, or the idea of a friend finding it and accidentally hurting himself or someone else makes me worried." You can share your emotional experience without even making a decision (for example, to get a pocketknife or not).

- **Demonstrate emotional availability.** Do this through things like making eye contact when your son says something, pausing to listen, and responding verbally not with advice but with "I can see how you would feel that way."

- **Be a secure, safe base.** Quite literally imagine yourself as the safe harbor for your son to leave from to explore and come home to when he wants.

- **Practice reflective listening.** When your son shares something, ask it back to make sure you understand his experience.

- **Empathize with and validate your son's feelings.** Do this by noticing, naming, and talking about feelings. For example, "You seem worried. Is that true? I can see how you would feel that way. This is a big test. Let's talk through how to manage worry you have felt in the past. What has worked before?"

- **Focus on building trust.** Strengthening attachment and attunement are important parts of developing a healthy emotional intelligence, and it starts with a trusting relationship.

- **Know when to walk away.** When your own emotions are rising, sometimes leaving the room is the healthiest choice. Always return to continue the conversation later.

- **Admit your failures.** Success is not a straight line. Share your own path of successes and failures—and validate the importance of failure in growth.

- **Teach self-soothing.** Help your son understand what works best for him. People relax and calm in different ways. Some like to go for a walk (active self-care) while others like to lie down and have alone time (quiet self-soothing). Some need help processing and talking through things, while others like to pause, step away from the crowd, and revisit the issue later. Help your son begin to know himself in this way. This information builds a self-care tool kit that he can readily access when things feel tough.

- **Teach the importance of breath.** The mind and body are closely connected. When the mind is heated, the breath can become shallow and rapid—and fast breathing is like adding fuel to a burning fire. Encourage your boy to slow things down: Breathe in for six seconds. Breathe out for six seconds. Repeat.

- **Teach problem-solving skills.** When people become emotionally flooded, it is hard to think through rational solutions to even the simplest problem. Having a simple strategy (like SWOCS) slows down the emotional process and gives structure to help think through the problem.

Stop.

What is the problem?

What are possible Options for solutions?

Choose the best option.

Ask yourself if you are Satisfied with your choice.

Being Present for Your Son

Attunement, attachment, and emotional intelligence are best supported through your connection with your son, and the quality of your attention makes all the difference. You want him to feel heard and seen, gain better clarity, and be ready to make positive change.

Here is an overview of how you can foster more secure attachment to raise emotionally healthy, feminist boys. Connection is built through *unconditional positive regard, empathy, validation,* and *mirroring.*

Unconditional Positive Regard

It is healing and feels good to be completely accepted by a person, regardless of what we say or do. Known as *unconditional positive regard,* its power has been studied for decades as a core element of psychotherapeutic change.[75] When parents offer it to children, this acceptance is known to have a positive impact on a child's mental health.[76] Kids need to feel like we love them just for who they are, not because of what they do. Acceptance is not dependent on how they behave, and it is not taken away when they make mistakes.

Here are some things you can say and do to demonstrate your unconditional positive regard for your son:

- When your child comes to you with difficult feelings and perhaps admits to something he did that went against family values, instead of immediately reprimanding the actions try to ask about his feelings and the thoughts behind the behavior. There will be time to talk about the actions later, but first show that you are here for him, that you want to understand him, and that you appreciate him coming to you.

- Don't make your affection tied to positive behavior or external measurements like good grades. Show your child that you love him no matter his behavior or report card. This does not mean you can't address the issues or behaviors later; it means that you first check yourself and make sure you're not sending the message that your love or positive regard is conditional.

- If you're butting heads with your child and the argument escalates, you can always let him know: "I love you even when I am upset. I just need a moment. Let's talk later." This shows your boy that even though you are angry, hurt, or upset, you still love him and that will never waiver. This is healthy management of difficult emotions. You are modeling how to take care of yourself and him during a heated discussion. This helps create an inner voice for your child that gives him the freedom to love himself as well.

Empathy

In parenting, we often advice-give. Scrap that. Very infrequently does someone want to be told what to do. Instead, focus on having *empathy* for your son's experience. When you have empathy for your boy, you see, understand, and feel his emotions—you're putting yourself in his shoes. It is an emotional experience rather than a cognitive one, as you can imagine what he might feel given his circumstances. The way you show empathy is by naming the emotional experience of another:

- Ask yourself, *What is the emotion my son is feeling?*

- Name it first for yourself internally.

- Then name it out loud to your boy: "I can see how sad that makes you."

  - If he says, "Yes, and…," just practice active listening.

  - If he says, "No, actually…," just say, "Tell me more. How are you feeling? I want to understand it completely."

- Then shut your mouth. It's easy to overspeak here. Less is more.

Showing empathy in this way is a simple approach to developing a strong connection.

Because you are attuned to your son's emotional experience, he feels heard and seen, and more connected and securely attached to you. You are a safe and a secure place to work from. Ultimately, these moments of empathic listening feel better for you and your son, and make a much bigger social change than you realize. You are redefining masculinity to include emotional experience, showing your boy that it's normal to feel and, more specific, encouraging him to become aware of what his feelings are.

Validation

In the step beyond empathy, *validation* is the recognition and acceptance of your son's emotional experience as true and valid. It doesn't mean you have to agree, just that you can accept and acknowledge that the feelings he has are true and real for him.

Say your son stomps around in a complete rage that his babysitter sent him for a time-out for throwing sand at his sister. As a parent, you might feel that the babysitter's response was reasonable and fair, but focusing on that invalidates your son's experience and isn't helpful. It is best to first validate his emotional experience. You might say, "I see you are so mad! It is so hard to have to go to time-out especially when you think your sister deserved it." This also buys more leverage, at a later time, when you can discuss other options aside from throwing sand.

Validation doesn't mean doing away with boundaries or rules. You can say, "If you throw sand, you have to take a time-out. I know that is so hard! You are mad! I hear you! I know some rules aren't any fun."

Set rules and expectations clearly, empathize and validate emotional responses at having to follow the rules, and focus on maintaining connection with your son during periods of pain. If you model validation, your son will grow to not only be able to empathize with another's emotional experience but also appreciate that it is valid and true, although he might not personally feel it. Imagine if all the men who committed sexual assault had this skill? The rates of assault would be significantly lower.

Mirroring

Children aren't born mean. Our sons aren't born rapists, yet many of them end up assaulting others. You can emphasize his positive traits by accurately reflecting your son's feelings and thoughts back to him through *mirroring*. You can act as a mirror for what he is saying or doing, which allows him to feel accepted, his experience to be validated, and his kind behaviors to be reinforced. It builds his genuine self-worth and value, as it helps him see the positive traits in himself.

Say your son reaches out to comfort a friend who is upset because he got in trouble at school. You would say, "You are such a kind and empathic person to see that your friend is hurting and then try to help." While your son might cognitively and instinctually know calling his friend is the right thing to do, through mirroring positive qualities you can help him see and internalize the positive attributes he exhibits, helping him build an internal framework that lasts a lifetime.

Knowledge and Skills

Strengthening attunement and secure attachment is the first part of raising a feminist boy. You can then build on this by educating him about policies, law, norms, history, and experience of women and other genders.[77] When boys are armed with knowledge, they feel more confident, clear about their own beliefs, more equipped to do something, have lower levels of hate, and have a stronger social justice perspective. When boys lack knowledge, they lack awareness and the ability to act—not because they don't care but because there isn't clarity about why sexist behaviors can feel "off" to them. You can step in and help your son put words and knowledge to what he feels inside.

Most children are born with an internal sense of equity and justice that is often socialized out of them. Don't let that happen. Validate the feelings your boy has and give evidence for why what he is sensing is wrong. As an example, you can say to your son, "I noticed you looked upset when you heard someone tell your sister she couldn't play a 'boy's game.' What were you feeling and thinking when you heard that? It's very normal to feel upset when you see some people being excluded or hear them saying words that are hurtful and untrue. It's wonderful that you care so much about your sister. Let's think through this together and find some ways you might be able to respond the next time something like this happens."

Awareness of Privilege

An empathic awareness of the daily lived experience and systemic oppression of girls, women, and other genders is necessary to be a true ally. It isn't enough to just understand this on a theoretical level, it is crucial that boys assess their own privilege and its impact on perpetuating this system.

Privilege is when people have unearned access to resources like food, housing, education, and job opportunities that many people are denied access to. For example, just being born in the United States offers more access to medical treatment and education than being born in a third-world country, and being born white significantly increases the quality of medical care and education. Being a white boy is privileged, as it offers more advantages than any other position in American society.

Let's take a look at some data to really bring the point home. When we look at salaries, who is getting paid the most? White men. Even in 2020, women earn eighty-one cents for every dollar earned by a man.[78] And when you factor in race, the situation only becomes more dire. "The largest uncontrolled pay gap is for American Indian and Alaska Native women, Black or African American women, and Hispanic women," who earn seventy-five cents for every dollar a white man earns.[79] Just by being born a boy, your son has unearned advantages, and he must understand the privilege in which he lives.

White privilege refers to having greater access to power and resources than people of color do simply due to skin color. For example, according to 2015 Census Data, the average net worth of an American non-Hispanic white household is $139,300, while that of a Black American household is $12,780.[80] White people in America are two to three times more likely to get approved for a mortgage than people of color.[81] If you want to see who gets to sit at the seat of power and influence, and make far-reaching decisions, look no further than our current 116th Congress. While it is lauded as the most racially and ethnically diverse Congress America has ever had, white non-Hispanic men make up 78 percent of voting members, which is more than the 61 percent share of the population white males occupy.[82]

White privilege also means having history books that record their experience of history, while leaving out or giving short shrift to the contributions of minority groups. And although many teachers acknowledge that Black history is important and relevant, only 8 to 9 percent of time in history class is devoted to teaching it.[83]

Privilege doesn't mean life is easy or that there aren't struggles, but it does mean your son has advantages based on his sex and perhaps his race. The more privilege someone has, the more power and protection they have. All it takes is a quick look at our criminal justice system, where "Black men who commit the same crimes as white men receive federal prison sentences that are, on average, nearly 20 percent longer."[84]

Take a look at what happened during the coronavirus pandemic. Who are the communities at greater risk of contracting or dying from COVID-19? It's communities of color who disproportionally shoulder this. According to the Centers for Disease Control and Prevention (CDC), ethnic and racial minority groups are at greater risk because of systemic health and social inequities such as long-standing discrimination, lack of health care access and utilization, housing challenges, and educational, income, and wealth gaps.[85] Being a rich white boy offers more inherent power and protection because of the way our society is organized and what we have historically valued.

To bring this awareness into his life experience, it helps to drop the veil and see how many experiences of privilege you both identify with. Do this together as you think through what privileges you have. This is not something to feel bad or guilty about, it is to recognize your positioning in the world and acknowledge it. This is feminism. Be self-compassionate and honest. The more you and your son understand in a true and authentic way, the freer he is to be an ally to others. There is not an "official privilege score" or way to quantify all of it. Instead, just look at what you and your son endorse, and think about where you fall compared to the rest of the world.

Talk about any of the following privileged statements that are true for him, and continue to probe how or why the statement is not true for all people. The purpose is to have the conversation and build awareness, not to come up with definitive answers.

I have enough money to not worry about food or shelter.

> Who doesn't have the money for food or shelter?
>
> Why might it be hard for people to earn enough money to eat?

I can easily access physical buildings and spaces. For example, I can get on a bus, go into the grocery store, and drive a car without physical limitations.

> Who can't easily get into this building and why is it designed this way?
>
> What modifications should be made to our spaces to be more accessible?

I have reliable transportation.

> How many people don't have reliable transportation and why is this the case?
>
> What does having transportation change in my life?

I am educated.

> Who helped you pay for an education and how were they able to help you?
>
> Who guided and taught you the steps you needed to get an education? What happens when someone else doesn't have those support systems?

I can afford to travel, at least some.

> How would your life look if you didn't have excess income for travel?
>
> What different choices would you have to make?

I am physically healthy.

> How different would your daily life be if you couldn't climb stairs, get around, or sit for long periods of time?
>
> What would happen if you got sick and didn't have insurance as a backup?

I am mentally healthy.

How different would your ability to do your job or schoolwork be if you weren't mentally healthy or able to get treatment?

How does your mental health affect your relationships and life decisions?

I speak English.

What would school have looked like for you if you didn't speak English?

How different would making friends at school be if you couldn't speak English?

I am American.

What are some of the securities you feel that come with being an American?

What would it feel like to have a different nationality and face immigration issues in America?

I am safe in my gender and sexual orientation.

How would you feel if the messages you received from the culture around you were that who you are is not okay?

What would change in your life if you felt your assigned gender didn't match your true gender?

I can share my identity and not have my safety challenged.

What would it feel like to know you couldn't tell anyone details about your parents' immigration status?

How would it feel to be worried about being deported at any time?

I am not worried about judgment, criticism, or exclusion based on who I am.

What protections are in place to make it so that you can easily speak your mind?

Who might face consequences for sharing their voice and why?

I am a boy/man.

When was the last time you worried about your safety, and how does being a man affect this?

Who might be more concerned about their safety on a daily basis and why?

I am white.

In which ways has being white made your life easier or opened doors?

How does white privilege benefit you, and who in return does this disadvantage?

I know this topic can feel heavy, and you may not know where to begin or how to have these types of conversations. The thing is, these are not one-off chats. They are meant to incorporate a broader worldview for yourself and your son. In almost every situation, there is someone not being included. Build the practice of noticing who.

Quite literally, on the playground there is always a child who wants to play but isn't or can't. At the beach, where I am renting a summer house, everyone is white. Why is that? At the neighborhood block party, everyone has a college degree—who isn't being included here and why? At the investment team meeting, all men sit around the table. How come? Begin to notice who is there—and who isn't there. And why. Help your sons notice too. That is step one.

Step two is asking yourself (and your son) how to make an environment more inclusive, accessible, friendly, and welcoming for everyone. How can you ask the left-out child at the playground if they want to play? How can you make the beach neighborhood or block party more accessible, equitable, and inclusive of all races? What barriers are in place that make people of color not able to be there or want to be there? At the investment team meeting, what needs to happen to have more women at the table and have their voices heard? In the end, it comes back to this: what can *you* do to bring about change?

These are big questions to tackle, and there is not one simple answer. But just noticing and asking is a step forward. Another place to start is by making friends who are outside of your usual (unconscious) parameters. Sign your kid up for a gym class in a community that has more people of color. Go to dinner at a place where you are in the minority. And be cautious about the statements you make about things and places that are different. I was recently driving through a low-income area with my son's friend, who said, "This area is creepy." He did not understand why, but my hunch is that he noticed the socioeconomic difference and felt outside of his comfort zone. Different isn't dangerous. Notice the feeling and be curious why you feel that way. Engage in a conversation.

I am cautious not to say I have this all down or I am doing it all right. The thing is, this is a process for us all, and I do not think we will ever be all the way there. Fundamentally, we are biased, and it creeps up in our life all over the place. But this is important to me, and I have seen the upside in my own home. A few proud mama moments were when my eldest asked if we could volunteer at a soup kitchen because he knows people have less than we do. Or when my daughter noticed a family with gay parents and she treated them like they were just another family. Or when my other son felt sad after the Fun Run because there were children who did not get any special prizes because they had not fund-raised enough.

Openness Fosters Support

When you reflect on your son's personality, is he imaginative, emotional, intellectually curious, sensitive, and creative? Or is he a boy who prefers routine, is more rigid, concrete, tuned out, and cautious? One is not necessarily better than the other, as these traits are on a spectrum. The first list indicates a natural openness to new ideas, which is a critical piece of being an ally. It is one domain in the Big Five Personality Model,[86] which includes characteristics on a spectrum from being inventive and curious to consistent and cautious. Traits of openness include imagination, sensory sensitivity, creativity, emotionality, and intellectual curiosity. If you're interested in seeing where you and your son land, use this online assessment tool: https://open-psychometrics.org/tests/IPIP-BFFM/.[87]

Openness is an essential characteristic in being an ally, as it allows our boys to hear someone's experience, be receptive to understanding, and learn something that is outside of their experience. If openness is not natural to him, you can help him practice being more open by asking the following questions:

- What would someone else (you can keep it vague or name a specific person) think in this situation?

- What would need to happen for you to be more willing to try new experiences, like making friends with someone different from you?

- I'm curious if there is something you are fearful about when it comes to trying new experiences. If so, what are you afraid of? Why? How can we work on that?

- What feelings come up for you when you learn about others' experiences?

- How can you practice feeling calm and centered while you hear about others' experiences, especially when they are painful to hear?

- In what ways can you learn about others by yourself? Through books, music, blogs, podcasts, documentaries?

Openness is linked to the two other domains, knowledge and awareness, as you have to be open to becoming aware in order to gain knowledge, which can then translate into actions like activism, speaking out, and doing something different from the status quo. It will help your son support all people.

Help Your Son Build a Clear Internal Compass

In psychology, we aspire for *integration*, which happens when what we think, feel, say, and do are all in alignment. Rather than having hugely polarized or competing parts of ourselves, we feel grounded, connected, and cohesive. Integration also means putting theory into practice.

The result of integration is that your son won't want to act like a bad guy if he sees himself as a good guy. When boys have clarity around who they are and solid values, they act as a solid internal compass to work off of. When they are in the locker room and a teammate starts talking about "finger banging" his friend, he will notice the discomfort in himself and understand that the discomfort is there because misogyny is against his value system. He will be more likely to speak up and say something different.

Because moving from skills to internalization to action is much harder if our boys don't have a clear sense of their core values, I encourage you to help your son clarify his values. Young-adult years are marked by a search for one's own identity and an understanding of where one fits in with the world. Helping your son from a young age to develop a sense of his own character values and to find what's important to him will give him an inner guide that'll last a lifetime. Labeling and defining these character values, and discussing moments when these could be tested or when your son has already been tested, can be very useful.

Ask him things like: "What does it mean to have courage, dignity, or honor? How do you show respect to others? How are you able to ask for respect for yourself? How do you feel when your thoughts and actions are aligned with your own values? How does it feel when they aren't?"

Here are some more questions that will translate the theory into action. They will help you build a parenting road map and, moreover, help your son understand himself and his values on a deeper, more conscious level through self-reflection, self-awareness, and self-compassion.

- What are five words you would use to describe yourself? What are five words others would use to describe you? Are they the same or different? Why?

- What are five words you would like to be described as by other people, even if they are not how you describe yourself now? What would you have to do differently for people to describe you this way?

- (To older boys:) When do you feel most like yourself? (To younger boys:) When do you feel happiest?

- What are you most proud of? Why? How does it fit with how you see yourself as a person?

- What are you least proud of [he can answer privately to himself or to you]? Why? How does it fit with how you see yourself?

- Fast-forward five years. What do you think will be most important to you and why? Fast forward to when you are an adult. What will be most important to you and why?

- Out of all your friends, who would you say is the "best person?" Why? How do you define "best person?"

- If you could do anything to make the world a better place, what would you do?

- Fast-forward to when you are one hundred years old. What qualities or values do you think you will be most proud of in yourself?

After discussing these questions, make a values list with your son. Write down what he most values: in himself, in family, in friends, in strangers, in community, in the country, in the world. Point out to him that these are the things that matter to him.

Now that your son has a clear sense of his values and is well under way to building his internal compass, he can focus on putting these values into action. Look at the values list with your son. Ask him to pick the top values, no more than ten, and then pose these questions.

- How can you remember these and apply them today, tomorrow, and every day?

- What is something you can tell yourself when you feel unsure of right and wrong? What questions can you ask yourself when you feel unsure?

- What can you do to refocus and try again when you have trouble matching your actions with these values? How can you stay true to these values and be self-compassionate?

Grab a notepad or a journal and make a list of how he'll put these values into action. He can keep this list with him as a reminder when he feels unsure. Encourage him to come back to this list and adjust as life teaches him by challenging him in the moment. If you are feeling inspired, download the Values Action Plan from this book's website, http://www.newharbinger.com/46677. Fill it out and hang it on your refrigerator to keep your son focused on his plan.

Feminist Takeaways

Much of building an ally and a solid internal compass is about modeling and raising awareness in our sons. Boys internalize thoughts and feelings from what you say and what you model. It is also critical to help them see themselves as authentically and honestly as possible.

When they are young, they are actively building emotional intelligence, which eventually translates into what we think of as morality, character, and integrity. Those aren't qualities someone is born with—they are built over time. The more your son can practice reflecting on his values and connecting them to his actions, the more likely he is to have higher emotional intelligence and therefore be happier and healthier. Happy and healthy boys are the best allies and can be the next generation of emotionally connected and self-aware men if you tweak the lens through which you parent and put this into focus.

CHAPTER 4

Talk Openly About Gender, Sex, and Identity

Conversations about gender and sexual identity support your boy's healthy development, benefit others, and help create a culture that is open, accepting, and positive. These conversations instigate social change. Being an ally means having knowledge, being open, and offering support, so modeling and teaching your son through self-awareness, clear language, and understanding of both yourself and others encourages your son to act on his values.

Don't worry. Parents get freaked out about talking about gender, sex, and identity. If you understand the importance but do not know where to begin, this chapter will help give you the tools you need to have honest, straightforward conversations with your son.

First, I'll share three communication tools, which are essential because the way you speak is tied to how accepted and loved your son feels. We'll then clarify the language you use so that your vocabulary is up to date and you can share the right words. I've also broken down the conversations into age-appropriate levels, so you know how and when to discuss topics.

The Inner Work of Communication

Before we get into logistics, let's frame the conversations. In every conversation remember to encourage: *self-reflection, self-awareness,* and *self-compassion.* Relating positively always starts with the self and solid connection, so we'll start this chapter the same way.

Self-Reflection

Self-reflection is our willingness to look inward and be open to learning about our self. With self-reflection, your son can separate himself enough from his thoughts and feelings to look internally, as if seeing himself from the outside. This is an important step toward becoming a feminist boy, as he needs to understand himself and his position in the world to be an agent for social change.

To foster this self-reflection, encourage him to set aside time to turn inward: at night while lying in bed and in the morning before starting his day. Have him consider questions like, "What have I done lately to show kindness to myself and others?" "What am I taking for granted that I should spend more time acknowledging?" or "Am I achieving the goals I'm setting for myself? What is blocking the way?"

Regular journaling is a powerful method of self-reflection. Encourage him to keep a journal in which he can write down his innermost, private thoughts—and respect that you do not need to read them. Get him excited about this ongoing conversation with himself by sharing what he'll get out of it: stress reduction, getting to know himself better, clarification of thoughts and feelings, more-effective problem solving, and being better equipped to resolve disagreements with others in his life.[88]

You can give him prompts to journal about. Some great questions that get writing and self-reflection going are:

- When do I feel most in tune with myself?

- If I could talk to my future self, what would I say?

- What are some of my favorite memories and why?

- What are qualities of myself that I like? What are ones I aspire to attain?

Self-Awareness

We engage in self-reflection in order to become more self-aware. Self-awareness comes after reflection. When we are aware of our thoughts, feelings, and behaviors, the qualities of our personality and individuality become clear to us. Self-awareness helps us align our behavior with our values. Most parents want to raise "good guys" but underestimate the power of cultural messaging. They underestimate the strength of the message around how boys should think, feel (or not feel), and behave—solely because they are boys.

Toxic masculinity, also known as traditional masculinity ideology, is a belief system about boys and men that shapes how boys see themselves and how others see them too. Although masculinity shows up in different forms within different populations (white masculinity is different, in some ways, than Latino masculinity), there are common themes across populations. For example, there are messages of anti-femininity, a focus on achievements, suppression of emotion, and the need to be tough, violent, risk taking, and adventure seeking.[89] Toxic masculinity puts our boys at higher risk for school discipline, academic problems, and health issues (substance abuse, suicide, and cardiac problems, to name a few). Because of this, in 2018, the American Psychological Association developed guidelines for working with boys and men around their masculinity and how it shapes their health and who they are as people.[90]

It is crucial that you consider how masculinity impacts your son, for his benefit and others'. If we expect our sons to help change the culture of toxic masculinity and be allies who acknowledge their own privilege, then they must have self-awareness. A self-aware boy notices the pull he feels in social groups and questions it. For example: "I feel myself wanting to join in the locker room talk. I wonder why? What do I truly need here? What will I achieve by participating, not participating, or speaking up on behalf of the person they're talking about?"

Boys need to practice self-awareness because, like muscles, awareness takes time to build up. At first, it will be easiest for them to pay attention to their self during times that are devoted to it, in short increments. Over time, boys will start to notice their feelings and thoughts in the moment, almost as if they are watching live theater inside their head. When we get to this point real change happens, because things that were unconscious have moved into the conscious mind.

To help foster this perspective, ask questions like these and then either have a conversation or encourage your son to write the answers in his journal.

- When you look back at your day, what are you most proud of? Why? How is it connected to your values?

- When you look back at your day, what do you wish you had done differently? Why? What would you have done differently?

- If you had to pick a highlight and a lowlight of your day, what are they? Why? How do these moments connect with who you are as a person?

- Pick something that was uncertain, unclear, or something you struggled with.

  What were your feelings?

  What were your thoughts?

  How did you respond? What was your behavior?

  How do you wish you responded?

  How does your response match with your values, how you see yourself, and how you want others to see you?

  Can you become aware of these feelings, thoughts, and behaviors in the moment as they happen?

- What did you do today to promote equality?

- What did you do today to be an ally?

  In what ways were you open?

  In what ways were you seeking knowledge about someone else's experiences?

  In what ways were you supportive of someone else?

Sometimes when our boys self-reflect and become more self-aware, they learn and grow but don't always like what they see. For example, acknowledging their privilege coupled with their lack of advocacy or action can make them feel guilty and ashamed, which shuts down learning, growth, and connection to others. As humans, we are a work in progress, and that is an important lesson to communicate to your son.

Self-Compassion

Rather than being judging and critical of ourselves during times of pain or failure, self-compassion allows us to be kind and understanding to ourselves.[91] Self-compassion helps boys see their shame and pain as part of a larger human experience instead of just a personal flaw or inadequacy. A boy with self-compassion acknowledges his struggles. Instead of hiding them, he says or thinks, "I'm pissed, I didn't do my best in that game. I know I can play better. There is always the next game."

Many boys, especially younger ones, won't connect their self-compassion to compassion for others, and that is okay. But boys who are self-compassionate are more likely to be compassionate toward others—practicing self-compassion builds the compassion muscle, in general. As your boy ages and as he understands the concept of privilege, it is important to teach him to not hide behind or ignore it. Give him the language though: "I know I have a lot of opportunities that others don't have. I don't have to feel bad about that, but I do have to recognize it, appreciate that a lot of what I do have is because I am a boy, and I will be aware of this and pay attention to make sure others are included and not left out." Give concrete examples. Help your son understand when other genders are left out, and connect what it would feel like to be left out or unable to do what he wants to do.

There are three components to self-compassion: *self-kindness* (vs. self-judgment), *common humanity* (vs. isolation), and *mindfulness* (vs. over-identification).[92]

Self-kindness: Teach your son to practice being kind to himself when something goes wrong or when he notices a part of himself that he doesn't like. *Parts language* works well here, taken from a psychotherapy theory called internal family systems (IFS).[93] IFS helps people notice, name, and accept competing parts of themselves or conflictual emotions. Here is a real example from a kindergarten boy: "There is a part of me that wants to be mean to one of the girls in my class. She is so annoying and kinda bad. The rest of the class is mean to her. There is also a part of me that knows I should be nice. It is hard when everyone is mean to you. It is okay for me to feel two different ways at the same time, and I will be nice because I know it is the right thing to do."

The "mean girl" happened to be the only Black person in the class. Although the boy saw her behavior and knew on some level that she seemed different, he did not yet understand intersectionality and why this little girl might be potentially acting out. As a parent, your job is to help your son notice the conflicting feelings, help him have self-kindness for these feelings, and assist him in making a choice that is in line with your family values of love, acceptance, and kindness.

Common humanity: Although feelings seem very personal, more often than not the emotional experience is shared by others. This can be a point of connection rather than distance. Teach your boy to accept that "If I feel it, others feel it too." This allows him to overcome the message from toxic masculinity that tells him to shut down emotion. When boys accept and move toward their emotional experience, and even express it or share it with others, they can experience a sense of connection in humanity's commonality. Teach your son that it is brave to notice his feelings, acknowledge them, and potentially share them with others. This allows others to accept their feelings, creates connection, and provides an opportunity to grow and understand these parts more.

Mindfulness: Simply put, thoughts and feelings are reactions to the outside world. Boys are sometimes flooded by emotions and thoughts. They can mistake a thought or feeling for a core part of themselves, as a reflection of their character, rather than just a neural experience to stimuli. Teach your boy to be mindful of how thoughts and feelings arise and pass on their own. Watch feelings like a passing storm. Our culture has historically shut down these parts of our boys, so when they can notice emotions coming and going in order to learn how to manage them, they're also positively impacting their community.

A Simple Thought-Watching Exercise

Teach your boy to *take a curious stance* around emotional experiences without judgment, to watch his thoughts and feelings as though they are playing on a screen. Ready to try it? Guide your son through this practice enough times that he can do it himself.

1. Find a quiet spot where your son can sit for five minutes.

2. Tell him to imagine sitting behind a waterfall. The water falling is a cascade of his thoughts and feelings.

3. Tell him not to judge what he sees. Just to separate from his thoughts and feelings, and notice them.

4. Ensure that he has a regular, even breath.

5. He doesn't have to do anything, just notice.

6. After five minutes, have your son applaud himself for taking part in an exercise that is good for his health and helps him understand himself better.

Mindfulness can help your son (and you) learn that he has control over things that often feel out of control. When thoughts and feelings seem to be pummeling down, this exercise helps separate your son from the chaos.

Speak the Same Language

Language reflects our culture. Check out the Glossary at the end of this book. Read through these definitions so you can establish a common vocabulary and better understand what you will be talking about. It's okay to fumble. Language changes. Own it, and make the effort.

During your conversations, it is really important to feel comfortable saying to your son, "I'm not sure about that. Let me find out, learn more, and get back to you." You can use the glossary as a trusted resource. You can also find more resources in the Reading Group Guide at this book's website, http://www.newharbinger.com/46677.

Tips for Having Conversations

What you say and do matter a lot. Your son is watching and listening. Be reflective, aware, and compassionate with yourself and him. Your love, connection, and acceptance is what matters most. The underlying communication should be that you accept and love your son unconditionally. You always love your son but don't always love his behavior—these are two separate things.

Share this message often and be careful not to say, "I love you so much, *but…*" The "but" undoes the love. Keep love and behavior completely separate. Don't say, "I love you so much, *but* I wish you dressed like the other boys, so you won't get teased." It is preferable to say, "I love and accept all of you unconditionally. Seeing you get teased is hard for me, and I always have your back. It is important to me that you are exactly who you are. We will get through this together."

This effort isn't *one* talk, it is *many* talks. Allow time for conversations about gender, sex, and identity to be ongoing, because your son may need time to warm up to them. Attempt conversation with your son and watch how he responds. If he resists and tries to break away, come back later. Don't force it. By trying to talk, he knows this is important to you and gets the message that you care. Keep trying. The sooner you start, the more normalized it is, making it easier for both you and your son. When you start conversations early and have them consistently, conversations on sexuality and gender identity become part of his development.

Create a space to talk, learn, and connect before discussing any behavior like dating, masturbating, kissing, or acting on attraction. First, focus on his inner experience (like his emotions, needs, and internal conflicts). Parents freak out when they hear about sexual or concerning behavior and fly into action mode. Pause, listen, and be curious about the emotion under the behavior. "Wanting to have sex (the behavior) is natural. How do you feel about sex with your girlfriend (the emotion under the behavior), and what makes you want to do it now?" Pause often and listen for his emotion. Always validate that first. Deal with the behavior later. More often than not, it is all within normal developmental expectations. Join your son in thinking through what's beneath the behavior together. This is most effective in behavior change.

Avoid any temptation for gendered talk like, "Boys should…" or "Girls are…" or "That is a boy activity…" Be especially cautious not to invalidate emotions based on gendered expectations with statements like, "Man up," "Act like a lady," or "Don't be so sensitive." All of these can unconsciously roll off the tongue because they are culturally ingrained and normalized. Raising feminist boys means changing your own messaging and the expectations you set, conscious or not, so take responsibility for your own biases, which you identified in chapter 1.

Encourage relationships with people of different genders. It is really important for feminist boys to have female voices in their lives, offering a different experience and perspective than their own. Offer opportunities to read about girls, women, and other genders through developmentally appropriate books, movies, and television shows.

Talking to Kids Ages 0 to 3

You might cringe thinking about talking to your baby about sexuality and identity, but these conversations should be ongoing and start early. With babies, begin by naming body parts with proper terms—part of this is to desensitize any awkwardness or discomfort down the line, for both you and him.

And this is also where you own self-awareness comes into play. Be thoughtful around the books, toys, and clothes you choose to buy him. Whether you use verbal language or not, you are constantly sending messages about gender identity. Now is the time to consider how you would feel if your child is not the assigned gender at birth, if he someday asks to be a she or someone else, or if he is attracted to men. What would that mean to you? You can create an environment now where your son feels safe, so as he gets older this feeling of safety continues, regardless of his gender identity and sexual orientation.

Talking to Kids Ages 3 to 4

Preschoolers are savvy little ones. Developmentally, they consciously and unconsciously absorb so much messaging around gender, identity, and sexuality. They notice differences between themselves (and their families) and others (and other families). Schools begin to divide classes by gendered activities, and boys start to get the message that it is more normal to play with other boys rather than with girls. They hear the message of masculinity loud and clear.

Preschoolers begin to notice differences between self and others, including who is in their family. Move toward these conversations and validate what your boy notices. You might say, "Yes, that family is different than ours. They have two moms and three kids (or whatever the case may be). Although they look different than us, they all love each other just like we do. It's great to have friends who are different."

It is also important for parents to look at who they choose as friends, since modeling is most influential. Look for friendship in lots of places, and show your son that you value difference. Promote friendships with different genders. Parents can talk all they want, but real learning comes from their peers.

This is also the age when kids start to say things like, "Boys do…" or "That's a girl toy." Challenge those assumptions and ask, "What makes that so? Does that make sense to you?" Help your son critically assess the assumptions and messaging he has absorbed. Give your boy as much choice as possible in his life by offering him opportunities to be in many different activities (acting, soccer, ballet, music). Instead of automatically signing him up for "boy activities," make his interests and passions a topic of conversation.

And while we're at it, this is a great time to start introducing age-appropriate housework and home chores to your son. These teach important life skills and also help break the association of more traditional gendered norms tied to specific household tasks such as cooking, cleaning, and folding laundry.

Talking to Kids Ages 5 to 10

During the elementary years, boys become much more social, socially aware, and independent. They filter cultural messaging through their own lens as they interact with more children and adults outside of the home. Parents still have a huge influence, but the messaging becomes broader and from many sources.

Kids at this age become clearer about their own identity. It is the beginning of boys starting to build a more solid sense of who they are—how they are similar to and different from their family and friends. When they do, it is a great opportunity for you to validate the difference and also name the similarities. Start to share more language around the differences they notice too, using the Glossary at the end of this book.

It is really important for parents to reflect back all the positive qualities they see in their son during this stage. Transgender and nonconforming kids become clearer about who they are during these years too and need extra support and validation around identity. About 1 out of 250 adults are transgender,[94] so create a climate of openness. No matter your child's gender identity and sexual orientation, it is really important to give him lots of choice around expression and preference. Ask your child what pronouns he prefers (he/his/him, she/her/hers, they/them/theirs). Use the gender pronouns your son wants and encourage him to do the same for others.

All of this can be difficult for parents. No matter how hard we try, we have a set of expectations for our children—how we picture their futures, weddings, partners, relationships, and life experiences. When our boys have different identities than we imagined, it can be a challenging adjustment. One thing to keep in mind is that this is something for you to sort out but should never be brought into the parent-child dynamic, as it can be psychologically damaging to your son at a vulnerable time.

These conversations will come up unexpectedly, so be ready to have them when they occur. It is okay to not have a perfect conversation and come back it to it later when you've had a minute to think about your response. It is also okay to say, "I don't know. Let's find out." The most important message to send is that you are comfortable with these conversations and that you welcome them. They are important now and will continue in importance as your boy faces bigger and more challenging concerns in middle and high school.

Be ready to give answers to specific questions that seem beyond his years, like, "What is rape? What is a blow job? What is sixty-nine? What is a pimp? Why do people sell their bodies for sex?" to name a few. Stay calm. Answer simply, concretely, and unemotionally. For them, it's just a question, so the cooler you play it, the clearer your message is that you can tolerate these types of conversations and that you're a good resource.

Afterward, make sure to ask, "Does that make sense to you? Do you have other questions?" If you are caught off guard, default to "Hmm. Let me think about that. Can we talk about it later today? Just give me a minute to remember and find out more."

This is when you can lay the groundwork for puberty. Start sharing books for your son to first peruse on his own, and then ask if he wants to talk and look through it together. Boys in elementary school might start to notice armpit sweat and smell, plus early-morning erections. Boys as young as six can experience this, so just be straight with him. "Is your penis ever hard when you wake up? Either way it is totally normal." By fifth grade or even earlier, some boys experience unwanted and often not understood erections at home and school.

Help your son understand his body: "Your body is getting ready for puberty—when you begin to transition to being a man. That means your body will change and your voice will deepen, you will get some body hair, and you'll start to get erections—which is when blood flows to your penis. All of this is normal and exciting!"

Help him think through what to do if he experiences an erection, like tuck it into his pants at school. He should also know that touching it feels good. It's normal but should be done in private (in his room or bathroom, not at school), and eventually it will secrete semen (which is also normal but just needs to be cleaned up properly with hand washing).

Try to take away the awkwardness by just imagining a bodily function you are teaching about. Remember, this is your discomfort—not his, if you start early enough. He might push back a little and laugh, but roll with it. You can even say, "I like talking about this stuff. It's kind of fun. And it's exciting—you are growing up right in front of me!"

Think of this as an exciting time. Your son is growing up and coming into his own in very real ways. Be a part of it, for your sake and his. Even in the busiest of lives, find time for emotional closeness and conversations. I still put my boys to bed and this is when we talk. Something about the end of the day with the lights off and no eye contact allow for really authentic and honest conversations.

Talking to Kids Ages 11 to 13

A hallmark of middle school is puberty. So much changes with our boys' bodies, relationships, and identities. It is really important for parents to stay connected and help inform the process, even if it seems as though our boys don't want to talk. They do. Stay close and keep the conversation open, honest, and frequent. Be direct. Be open. Boys might be spending more time in their room and exploring their body. That is okay. Give them space and validate their needs. You might say, "It is normal for you to want to explore your body more and touch yourself. Touching your penis will begin to feel really good, and that is an exciting part of getting older. Although it feels really good, it is something we do in private."

Boys are asking themselves, *Who am I? What do I like? Who do I like?* Knowing this, ask yourself how you can help in the way that best meets your son's unique needs. It is normal for boys to be exploring and questioning their sexual orientation now, and it is normative for them to even start "dating," although that may be different than you imagine—texting, some conversation, and very little sexual contact, if any. These romances are often short lived. It is a good opportunity for parents to be curious and interested in their boy's "love life" without judgment or agenda, as it lays the groundwork for bigger conversations in bigger relationships later. This is the practice round for you and your son. Be cautious not to romanticize relationships with girls, as you are indirectly sending the message that that is what you expect and want. Again, take a curious, accepting stance.

Send the message that your son deserves love, support, and respect in all relationships he has—regardless of gender or sexual orientation. Be clear too that there is an expectation for him to treat people with respect and kindness, even if he has trouble understanding or connecting with someone. He doesn't have to like everyone, but he has to treat them with respect as a fellow human. Teach your son to speak up for injustice, connecting him with his budding internal compass. When he feels something is "off" or "wrong," teach him to trust that compass and speak up.

If your son begins questioning gender or sexual orientation, he needs extra support. Empathize, validate, and tune in to his emotional needs. Be present and curious about his experience, and resist the urge to offer advice or problem-solve. Also, show respect for who your son wants to talk to about his gender, sexuality, and identity—even if it's not you.

He may ask things like, "How do people know who they are attracted to?" Or, more often than not, kids feel safer talking about their friends' questions or experiences rather than their own. So be open and accepting of their "friend's" orientation, gender, question, and exploration. Empathize with the emotion your boy describes in his friend (endeavor to say, "It is so normal to want to explore parts of himself at this age—who he likes and who he is") rather than the behavior (avoid saying, "I think your friend is too young to date").

Know what media your son is using, and talk with him about the messaging he may be receiving. At this age, boys start listening to different music artists that can be offensive. Don't just ban and lock down material you find "inappropriate." Be in the know, be curious about why he likes it, ask him if he hears the lyrics the way you do (in terms of why it is concerning or uncomfortable), brainstorm with him about how to handle it, and be clear about your expectations of him as a boy and human (and how he treats others—including his language and behavior).

Stay connected. There are no hard and fast rules here. And don't forget to celebrate how great it is to be a boy! There is so much about him to love! Help him understand that and see it in himself!

Talking to Kids Ages 14+

Adolescence is when some parents expect the sex and identity talk to start. Good news: if you are reading this book and you have a little one, you have done a lot of front-end work! If you are reading this book with a high schooler, don't freak. You have a little catching up to do, but the most important messaging remains: demonstrate open, informed communication, unconditional love, acceptance, emotional empathy, and validation.

Your son is already armed with an arsenal of information. Your job is to help sort accurate information from the rest, so he has everything he needs to make informed decisions as he navigates away from you, toward adulthood.

Individuation is when adolescents move away from their parents and develop their own path and trajectory. This is a normal, healthy process and one that scares parents. They feel the distance and loss of control of their baby, in some way. For boys in particular, they often "go dark," which means they are hard to reach, leaving parents wondering if they will ever come back. Spoiler alert: they always do.

The work here is to be a consistent, accepting, open sounding board while you permit the distance and the healthy process of separating from you as your teen explores and works on securing his identity. Remember, you want him to launch from you eventually—to go out into the world as a healthy, self-sufficient adult. He needs practice before that happens. Adolescence is preseason, or the time to test separation with training wheels. Be present and respectful of your son's needs and boundaries. Trust the process.

Exploration is part of this process. He is out on a mission of humanity—building a sense of who he is, what his limits are, and getting feedback from the world around him—what works and what doesn't. This can be painful for parents to watch. Poor decisions, bad relationships, and social landmines seem to be around every corner. But this is part of the process. Be by his side, as he needs you. You aren't his mission partner, you are the safe base to return home to when he chooses. Be ready to welcome him with open arms and help him think through strategies on his own mission. Continually calling him back and guiding too much just gets in his way and can actually make him more vulnerable. Be clear of your role here, as it changed from when he was little.

With separation and exploration come a lot of identity work and social navigation. This can be a real opportunity for connection with your son, so approach it with curiosity, empathy, and kindness.

Be alongside your son, not dictating his moves. It is wonderful to lay out potential options and help him make choices. For example, "I know you want to go to that party with alcohol. Let's think through your options: 1) not go, 2) go and not drink, 3) go and drink a lot, 4) go, carry a beer around, and sip it slowly all night. Let's go through the upside and downside of all options and make a plan." Empathize with the pressure your son feels in this social situation. Help him think through his social-emotional needs and wants, and brainstorm how to get those met in the safest way.

Parents often get scared of behavioral exploration (drinking, sex, and so forth) and try to control their son's behavior, which often shuts him out of the process and is not successful at deterring the actual behavior. This doesn't mean anything goes. It means being clear around reasonable family rules and expectations (that are regularly discussed), and helping your son navigate his personal, familial, and social needs. Be patient and thoughtful. This is tough for an adult, never mind an adolescent whose brain isn't even fully developed yet.

Human brains aren't fully developed until age twenty-five or so. This means that the part that is responsible for long-term planning and under-standing the repercussions of action is still developing. Help your teen under-stand that what feels so true in the moment is very real in that moment, but that it can also change quickly based on how his brain is currently wired.

That doesn't meet the feeling is invalid, it means he has to have an awareness of this and how he might feel the next day.

On the other hand, certain things don't often change over time—like gender identification and sexual orientation. Gender and sexuality is fluid, but we know trans and LGBTQI+ (lesbian, gay, transgender, questioning/queer, or intersex) kids often know their preferences early on, and they persist over time—they are "persistent, consistent, and insistent," which is a common mantra in helping parents determine what is a phase versus what is foundational identity.

Feminist Takeaways

If you got to this point in this book, you have all the foundation you need to get started with conversations—yes, a series of talks. Remember this is not a one-shot deal. This is an ongoing part of what you chat with your son about. You have the language, you learned about where your son is developmentally, and you have some key phrases to help navigate conversation.

All of this is important, but what really matters is your love. When in doubt, default to empathy, validation, unconditional love, and acceptance, and your relationship will flourish—and so will your son.

CHAPTER 5

Teach Physical Respect and Consent

When you think about your son, most likely you're flooded with wonderful memories of him playing with his friends, his adventurous spirit, uncontainable joy, and laughter. Sure, he can test your limits and make mistakes sometimes, but overall he's a good kid. It can be a difficult stretch to pause and consider if your son could ever push someone beyond their sexual or physical limits. Could he ever, in a moment of lapsed judgment, or under the influence of a substance or peer pressure, make the wrong choice?

This is a hard question to ask yourself of your own son. With one in five women having experienced completed or attempted rape[95] and 90 percent of sexual assaults being committed by men,[96] we can see why being a "good boy" just isn't enough. Boys are confused about the basics of assault and consent. In a national survey of eighteen- to twenty-five-year-olds, 32 percent of males either agreed or were neutral about the view that if "a woman does not physically fight back, it's not sexual assault."[97] Let that sink in. If boys do not understand the basics of assault and consent, then how will they know when they hear it, see it, or commit it?

Boys are confused. Despite being a mom who tries to talk about issues of gender, emotion, and equality, I still see it in my boys. Fresh off of YouTube or TikTok, Tyler easily falls into reciting misogynistic lyrics he does not even realize are dangerous and distancing—after all, they are just in a song all of his friends listen to. He struts around with his skater hair and tough-guy vibe, only to hop into bed with me at night, as he is scared of the dark and sleeping alone. He aspires to be a tough guy on the playing field but doesn't see the paradox of how sweet and gentle he actually is. At his baseball games, he is embarrassed when I hug him or cheer. He doesn't want to be a "mama's boy" after all. But he is. He's my little guy and would much prefer to stay home and hang out with our family than head out to a friend's house.

On one side, they're told about all the traits they need to exhibit to "be a man," thus leading them down the path of toxic masculinity. And on the other side, they're told what men do is horrible. "Be strong and brave," our culture says, "but your touch is dangerous." When journalist Peggy Orenstein interviewed several boys about what they liked about being a boy, most of them drew a blank. One of them responded with, "That's interesting. I never really thought about that. You hear a lot more about what is *wrong* with guys."[98] We need to completely change the way we view masculinity.

In this chapter, we'll dive deep into what boys are told about being a man, how it makes them feel, and what you can do to better guide your son at any age. Together, we'll equip your son with the knowledge and skills needed to understand the importance of consent, respecting boundaries, noticing and honoring "gut" feelings, and building character traits to help him step up when he knows something isn't right.

Now that you understand the importance of intentional modeling and ongoing conversations about physical respect and consent, we'll investigate the cultural conditions we're up against as we raise feminist boys.

Messages About What Masculinity Is and Isn't

Our boys are constantly receiving messages about who they are, how they should act, and who they should aspire to be. So, what is the consensus on what it means to be a "real man"? Adults say the most highly valued traits of men are honesty, morality, ambition, and leadership.[99] However, boys are much more likely to say that strength and toughness are the most valued by society. Only 2 percent of boys say honesty and morality.[100]

The reason for this disconnect is clear. We don't need to look far to see toxic masculinity's pervasiveness in society. Boys are told to "suck it up" or "be a man" when they feel scared or sad. Seven in ten boys say they feel pressured by parents, friends, teachers, and society at large to be physically strong.[101] Boys begin to form the belief that the ideal man is athletic, aggressive, stoic, domineering, and rugged, and that this is the epitome of sexual prowess. A 2018 national survey of more than a thousand ten- to nineteen-year-olds showed that while young women believed there are many ways to be a girl, young men described only one narrow route to successful masculinity: emotional suppression at all costs, except combative anger when upset.[102] These societal pressures are internalized to such a degree that boys begin to believe the only way to be a man is to exhibit signs of strength and toughness, which culminates in violence. Many cultural forces are defining this narrow route for our boys and furthering gender inequality in the process. Here's one example.

While Boy Scouts of America conjures images of campfires, canoes, and outdoor adventures, for many it also brings up gender inequality. It's assumed girls just aren't "tough enough" to kick it with the boys. Recently, the Boy Scouts of America have allowed girls to join, and the first female Eagle Scouts class was be recognized in 2020.[103] While this is a great step in the right direction, Sarah Rich, the author of "Today's Masculinity Is Stifling," asks a deeper and more unsettling question: Why aren't any boys asking to join Girl Scouts? Girl Scouts' merit badges tend to focus more on community, friendship, and caretaking, which are all things our culture lumps into feminine domains. Why aren't boys also being encouraged to care about their communities, friendships, and relationships?

Even though many people give lip service to gender equality, when you truly dive deeper, the old ways of gender norms are still staunchly present. In a 2018 poll, while 92 percent of adolescents said they believe in gender equality, 54 percent agreed that they are more comfortable with women carrying out traditional roles in society, such as caring for their children and families.[104]

Toys are especially gendered. Next time you're in a store, take a look at all the toys, clothes, school supplies, baby gear, and food items geared toward specific genders. Sociologist Elizabeth Sweet studies gender in twentieth-century children's toys and has found that we are now even more rigidly separating the genders than ever before.[105] "Toymakers are saying, well, we can sell each family one toy, or if we make separate versions according to gender, we can sell more toys and make families buy multiples for each gender."[106] This trend is concerning since consumer products have a serious influence over identity development and how we present ourselves.

The boys who play with strictly "masculine" toys, eat "man" food, and associate colors with gender grow up to be men who believe that if they use a product considered feminine, it is a direct threat to their gender and identity.[107] How many men would feel comfortable wearing women's perfumed deodorant? How many men would go to work with painted fingernails? How many men carry purses with them on their errands? These are all examples of ways that products have been marketed to specific genders, reinforcing the notion of what it means to be feminine or masculine.

As consumers, we can be more aware of the way product manufacturers appeal to and reinforce gender norms. Every time we purchase something, we in essence are casting a vote. While I'm not saying you can never buy a doll or truck or princess tiara again, I am saying that we as consumers need to be aware of the power we have when we purchase items and of what messages we are sending our children through the products we buy. If I only buy my boys typically masculine toys (like aggressive video games) and not follow up by buying the pink Vineyard Vines that Ty wants, I am sending a message: I see being a boy as tied to typically masculine products. Furthermore, it is important to acknowledge and support him stepping out of the norm by saying something like, "I love your hat. It is super cool and looks great on you!"

Looking for examples of toys and games that are active and non-gendered? Consider a trampoline. I know people have very mixed feelings about them, but we have two. They are the neighborhood hangout for the mixed-gender group of kids ages two to thirteen. It's where they all pile on, sit around, make up games, and look out for each other. Parents are always surprised to see how groups like this self-regulate when parents step back. They even have their own small sociopolitical system.

Board games—checkers or Connect Four are family favorites, and our kids also love doing arts and crafts and science experiments together. I have a hard time coming up with my own, so thankfully there are pre-boxed (although overpriced) science experiments the kids love.

Finally, my favorite thing to do with my children does not involve a toy at all: cooking together. Everyone lends a hand, we create something yummy to share, and we learn and experiment as we go. My whole family participates.

When Jokes Are a Language of Harm

The words we use and how we use them matter. A lot. The strongest correlation of boys feeling pressured to be physically strong and ready for violence is their exposure to sexual comments and jokes about girls.[108] Six in ten boys hear other boys make sexual comments or jokes about girls at least once a week.[109] This number bumps up to once a day for 36 percent of fourteen- to nineteen-year-old boys;[110] nearly half also said they heard their father or other male family members make sexually explicit jokes or comments about women.[111] Let's think about this. What is being said around your son right now, whether by family members, friends, or classmates? How does your son react to comments or jokes of a sexual nature?

The more frequently boys hear this language, the more they fall into toxic masculinity's grip. Two out of three boys between fourteen and nineteen have at least one friend who has asked a girl to send him sexy or nude photos.[112] One of the strongest factors correlated with thinking it's okay to ask girls for sexy or nude photos is having a father who has made comments or jokes of a sexual nature about women.[113]

While we're on the topic, let's put dads (and other adult men) on the hot seat for a minute. Raise your hand if you're a father and feel like boys are just going to be rough and tumble and need to be raised completely differently than girls. Maybe you think they need a ton of sports in their lives or that they need to learn how to do the "man jobs" around the house. Or maybe you even tell your son when you're leaving town for work that he needs to take care of his mom since he's the "man of the house now."

It's time for dads to really reflect not only about what they believe to be true about their son's masculinity but, even more important, about their own. Where do these notions of what it means to be a man come from? How deeply rooted are these beliefs? What would happen if you changed your views? How do you think others would react, and what are your fears, worries, or concerns about how others would react? What feelings would this bring up in you, and how would you work through them in a healthy way?

Again, raising feminist boys doesn't (necessarily) mean raising feminine boys, it means raising boys who believe in equality for all and do not separate themselves from others based on the power and privilege handed to them. Taking care of Mom is a wonderful thing for all kids to think about and appreciate—not just your son. Holding doors open, treating others with respect, and taking responsibility for things that you can are all important life skills for children—not just our boys.

It's time for dads and others to pay attention to the language being used around our boys and to have direct conversations with them, so boys have the internal fortitude and conversation skills to stand up for women. Otherwise, they'll turn into young men who say "I hit that," "I nailed it," or "I crushed that" using violent and degrading language to mark sexual conquests.

Emotional Repression Leads to Outbursts of Rage

"Boys don't cry," "Man up," and "Stop being a pussy" are all common phrases meant to induct boys into the "man code" and effectively teach the importance of hiding and masking their emotions. Our current society pressures boys from a young age to find alternative ways to deal with emotions. By the time boys reach adolescence, says Harvard psychologist William Pollack, boys become "shame-phobic" and are convinced that they will lose peer respect if they share feelings and personal problems.[114] Oftentimes, these repressed feelings can express themselves outwardly as aggression and anger.

So, boys learn to suck it up. They don't cry. They don't confide in other boys or men. When they do confide in anyone, it is usually mothers, girl-friends, and sometimes sisters.[115] While on the exterior it may be nice to know that boys and men at least have someone they can go to with their emotions, it also continues gender inequality by placing the burden of emotional labor squarely on women's shoulders. It teaches boys that emotions are women's work. That they don't need to find ways to handle their own emotions better and that it would be emasculating to even try. Not being able to identify, show, or know how to process their own emotions in healthy ways sets boys up to be ill-equipped for future meaningful and lasting adult relationships.

While men have been conditioned to handle their emotions through demonstrations of dominance and aggression, women have learned to placate men out of fear of harm. As Margaret Atwood so poignantly stated, "Men are afraid women will laugh at them. Women are afraid men will kill them."[116] The ever-present unspoken threat of violence of repressed feelings that men bring to sexual interactions takes a very real and serious form for women. Pair these repressed feelings with boys not understanding the basics about consent and assault, and we can see how we have gotten where we are as a culture.

Our children are left to shape their views of sexual relationships based on what they see in the media of male sexual entitlement and female sexual availability. Unfortunately, this leads to a whole group of boys who grow up never thinking they are a part of the problem. After all, they're "good guys," right? As one college junior said, "It's always someone else that's the bad guy, so you never think about addressing something that doesn't concern you."[117]

We know that assault among adolescents is more likely to be a crime of opportunity whereby "boys do it because they can: because they are oblivious, because they are ignorant, because they are impulsive, because they have not learned to see girls and women as fully human."[118] Boys who grow up never having conversations about respecting boundaries, consent, or physical respect therefore grow up to be entitled and blind to the world thinking they could never be part of the problem—so why bother looking too closely?

Never Stop Having Conversations

Even if you are the parent who has talked to your son about the mechanics of sex and protection, the vast majority of boys say that they've never had a single conversation with their parents about how to be sure a partner wants to have sex, is comfortable having sex with him, or what it means to be a respectful and caring sexual partner.[119] Two-thirds had never been told they shouldn't have sex with someone who is too intoxicated to give consent, and 67 percent had never had conversations with their parents about the importance of not pressuring someone to have sex with them after they said no.[120]

We parents can do better. We must do better. Our boys are not likely to change their mindsets and truly understand the gravity of the issues surrounding consent without active engagement in candid conversations.

Based off what we know from previous chapters as well as our own lived experiences, having just one talk about sex from your parents isn't going to cut it. The key to having a lasting impact is to have discussions often and early in an age-appropriate way. Conversations don't need to be cringeworthy. You can encourage discussions in an informal way. The next time you're watching a movie or television series with your elementary-age son and you hear something that speaks about women in a derogatory way, stop the show. Ask your son if he noticed it. How does that make him feel? Why would they have added this in the movie? Who does it harm?

The other week, I was in the car with my son and "Blurred Lines" by Robin Thicke came on. We both naturally started singing, and then I became more conscious of the words that just slipped off my tongue. I knew I had to help him identify the misogyny. We broke down the lyrics together and I asked my son to explain the words to me. What does it mean to domesticate a woman?

"I have no clue."

I said, "Think about it. What else is domesticated?"

He said, "Animals. That is weird."

We went on to have a conversation about why they were portraying women as animals needing to be liberated by men. The more you can dive deep and make space to reflect and discuss the messages our everyday culture sends out, the better equipped your son will be to see it for what it is when he's out on his own. Although understanding the meaning is important, pausing, becoming aware, and challenging messaging that somehow glides into our subconscious is the most important thing. I want my son to be a critical consumer of everything and have an awareness that so much of what we absorb goes unchecked. It is our responsibility to check as much as we can.

Explaining What Consent and Assault Are

Let's clear up boys' confusions about what consent and assault are. *Consent* is an agreement between participants to engage in sexual activity—which might seem like a buzzkill when you imagine being in the heat of the moment. But, it doesn't have to be. First and foremost, consent is a communication. Every time.

Consent is about setting his personal boundaries and respecting the boundaries, limits, and desires of his partner. Your son needs to know if and to what extent a potential partner wants to be sexual with him. He needs to be honest with himself and the partner about what he wants and doesn't want. If these things aren't clear, consent is about checking in with himself and his partner. If we end here, you might think, "Of course this makes sense, but I cannot picture my awkward teenager politely asking to touch a breast or body part every step along the way." But consent and communication is not just a business deal, it can be hot.

In the best-case scenario, sex can be empowering, connecting, and fun. A random, fast hookup might be hot in the right situation, but the reality of it is that most of these types of encounters fall flat. Think back to your own history. Think about the hottest sex you have ever had. It was probably with someone who was connected to you, caretaking in some way, and maybe verbal.

Teach your son that being a good lover is giving and receiving, and a big part of that is knowing what his lover likes. Teach your boy to ask and build it into the sexual experience. Teach him to know what he likes, find the words to say it, and ask his partner the same, including what they like doing in that particular moment. He can say, "I love getting kissed on the back of my neck. What is your favorite? What would you like me to do now?" Although he doesn't have to spell out each and every sexual experience, your boy needs to be concretely taught that consent has to be freely given (not persuaded), it is always reversible for all parties, and it is informed, enthusiastic, and specific.

Consent can be easily remembered by the acronym of FRIES.[121]

F - Freely given

R - Reversible

I - Informed

E - Enthusiastic

S - Specific

Freely given: Consenting is a choice you make without pressure, manipulation, or under the influence of drugs or alcohol.

Reversible: Anyone can change their mind about what they feel like doing, anytime. Even if they've done it before, and even if they're both naked in bed.

Informed: You can only consent to something if you have the full story. For example, if someone says they'll use a condom and then they don't, there isn't full consent.

Enthusiastic: When it comes to sex, you should only do stuff you *want* to do, not things that you feel you're expected to do.

Specific: Saying yes to one thing (like going to the bedroom to make out) doesn't mean you've said yes to other things (like having sex).

Once he knows what consent is, it's important to have conversations to further understand who can give consent. Can someone who is drunk give consent? How does age play into consent? How can you tell if someone is pressured to give consent? These questions must be asked and can lead to wonderful opportunities for both you and your son to really grapple with difficult questions.

Now let's take a look at defining assault. We know that many adolescents don't understand the range of behaviors that constitute assault. While assault is often defined as inflicting physical harm onto another person, there is another component, which is the actual threat or attempt to commit such an action. Sometimes the definition of assault includes an "intentional act that causes another person to fear that (they are) about to suffer physical harm."[22] This expansion of the definition helps police officers intervene before the victim is physically harmed. It can also help your son understand that assault can look like a wide range of behaviors.

Walk through examples and scenarios with him, and let these discussions help solidify his understanding of what consent and assault look like in different situations. Naturally, my kids play with this boundary—and it is my job to help them recognize where it lies. I do find that allowing some of the wrestling (mostly outside and on the trampoline, which I commonly refer to as the "pediatric fighting cage") allows them to focus on learning the non-verbal communication of when enough is enough. This is an active learning process whereby I help them learn to read the room, know their audience, watch their sibling's body language, and listen to what is being told to them. These nuances are the difference between a fun and friendly interaction and one where someone gets seriously hurt—now or in the future. In the current culture, we squash any whiff of physicality. In my opinion, that is a disservice.

If wrestling is beyond your comfort level or what you have for space (the noise makes me want to jump out of my skull, so they have to take it outside), the same theory can be applied to any and all play. The long and short is back off a little. Trust kids' instincts to work it out, and be by their side if they get stuck or need a hand.

Share Emotional Skills for Relationships

A large number of young adults end up completely unprepared to develop long-lasting, caring, and meaningful relationships. A study conducted by Harvard's Making Caring Common Project showed that 70 percent of eighteen- to twenty-five-year-olds wished their parents had talked to them more about emotional aspects of romantic relationships. Your son wants to know how to begin a relationship, how to develop a mature relationship, how to deal with breakups, and how to avoid getting hurt.[123] So talk to him about these things and share what you have learned.

The good news is that you can also do this with your own behavior, showing your boy what a healthy relationship looks like. Healthy relationships are built on trust, communication, mutual respect, honesty, patience, understanding, and safety. Ask yourself if you are modeling these in your current relationship with your partner and children. How are each of these qualities of a healthy relationship being expressed? How are they being received? What are some aspects of your own relationship you would like to work on to be a better model for your child? When there is conflict, how do arguments and reconciliation play out in your household? You are modeling, whether you are aware of it or not. Do what you can to model healthy relating.

You may not think of modeling healthy touch, but this is an essential way to convey how to share affection while respecting boundaries. A fifteen-year-old son won't want to cuddle with you the way a five-year-old will. It can be hard to know how to show affection to your ever-changing son, but loving touch is an important component to a healthy relationship.

From the time your son was a baby, you held him, rocked him, and kissed his forehead. While it may be easy to think your older son no longer wants or needs those hugs, nothing could be further from the truth. Loving touch is needed at every stage of our lives to foster healthy emotional and neurobiological development. Parents are in a unique position to model healthy touch from birth on for their child and show that healthy and caring relationships feel good.

Tips for Teaching Physical Respect and Consent

Teaching consent starts young and lays the groundwork for respecting physical and emotional boundaries throughout their lifespan. The earlier boys know this, the more likely they will be to have successful relationships, keeping themselves and others safe.

Skills for Ages 0 to 4

Children need to be taught that their comfort level and decisions about their own bodies will be respected. Teach your child from a young age that he is in control of his own body by respecting his physical boundaries.

- When he pulls away from a hug, let him go.

- When he says to stop tickling him, immediately stop.

- Ask whether he likes it when you stroke his hair.

- Do not tell your child he has to hug or kiss Grandma if he doesn't want to.

- Model consent to your child by asking for permission before washing him in the bathtub.

Respect your child's bodily independence and his decision on what is and isn't comfortable for him. This may mean having a conversation with your extended family about why hugs are not always given and that no one should pressure your child to give hugs. Honor his request not to be hugged or touched if he expresses it.

Give your child opportunities to say yes or no in everyday choices, whether it's the clothes he wears or how he fixes his hair. This gives him a sense of control over his own body and teaches him how to vocalize his preferences. In situations where you must step in for safety reasons (for example, if he wants to cross the street alone), make sure to explain to him that his voice matters and that you heard him, but that there are times when you as the parent need to step in to keep him safe.

Talk about "gut feelings" or his "belly voice." Help him recognize when he's feeling uncomfortable or weird or nervous, and that this "belly voice" is there to help him know when he is uncomfortable. Learn to recognize and label it.

Label body parts correctly instead of using code words (for example, say "penis" instead of "pee pee"). This helps break down stigmas, builds confidence in discussing his body parts with parents, and equips children with the language needed to better report sexual abuse.

Teach your child that when people use words like "no" or "stop" or "enough," their boundaries should be honored. When your child does hurt someone, teach empathy by explaining how a behavior led to the hurt. Encourage your child to imagine how he might feel if that was done to him and what he might do to help the other person in this situation.

Get your child used to observing behaviors and checking in on what he sees. This could be as simple as observing the family pet, siblings, friends, or parents. You might ask, "How are they feeling today? What clues do you see that leads you to believe that?" Teach your son to help other children when they are in need. Teach him to look for opportunities to help. When can he help a neighbor, a friend, his sister? Give him chances to build character values and feel good about caring for and helping others.

Skills for Ages 5 to 10

Show your willingness to talk about sensitive subjects with your child in a positive and honest way. The way you talk about his body changing, whether it's losing a tooth, developing acne, or getting an erection, will show your child that there is no shame or embarrassment in talking about these things and that he can always come to you.

Model active listening and show your child that no matter how difficult a topic he brings to you, you can respond to him in a calm and honest manner. This will help set the stage for your child to know he can confide in you with bigger issues in the future.

Encourage your child to be observant. Help him interpret what he sees happening on playgrounds or at school. You can ask him how some of those interactions made him feel. What could he have done differently?

Teach your kid to stop his play sometimes to check in on how everyone's feeling, including himself. This doesn't have to take long, but it is a good way to practice the skills needed for healthy relationships and issues of consent. Help teach your child that his behavior affects others. Ask him to observe how other people respond to something he did or didn't do. What will happen as a result of his actions and how did that affect other people's feelings? How does that affect your child's feelings after seeing the results his behavior had on others?

Skills for Ages 11 to 13

Middle school is a confusing time, and your son might be getting less-than-reliable information from all sorts of sources. Emphasize the importance of talking to a trusted adult. Remind him that he can always come to you or another trusted adult with any questions. Make sure you're ready to receive those questions and can answer him in a calm and nonjudgmental way. The more you can show your child that you can handle anything he brings to you, the more he will entrust you with his concerns.

This is when you need to clearly define terms like "consent," "sexual harassment," and "assault." Continue having talks about sex but start incorporating more information about consent. Discuss the following questions: How do you know if your partner wants to kiss or touch you? How could you tell if the other person is interested in you? How would you know if they aren't? How do you know if you're pressuring someone? In order to best prepare him to be a respectful, considerate, and caring feminist boy, share these ways to ask for consent:

"May I kiss you/touch you/take off your shirt?"

"Is it okay if I [insert desired action]?"

"What would you like me to do next?"

"Should I keep going? Or stop?"

"How far do you want to go?"

Educate about different types of touches. This is an age when many boys begin to play various versions of "touch games," like slapping butts or each other's genitals. Get kids talking about the impact those actions have on others. You might ask, "Do you think the other kid likes it when you do [insert behavior]? How might it make the other kid feel? How would it make you feel if someone did that to you?"

Help guide your child in identifying healthy and unhealthy relationships. Discuss examples your child might be familiar with in your own family or community, or on TV or film. What makes those relationships different from one another? Talk about what it means to be an ethical person. What does it mean to have dignity and respect for others? How do you intervene and advocate for those who are vulnerable or at risk of being harmed?

Skills for Ages 14+

Discuss hypothetical scenarios with your son regarding sexual harassment and assault. What does he see that is problematic? What would he do differently? Share stories of survivors. It can be incredibly powerful to see the real consequences of sexual assault. What does he learn from the situation? Will he do, act, and feel differently after hearing stories from survivors? Help your son analyze and identify the feelings that contributed to a violation of another person's sexual boundaries. Were there emotional or behavioral red flags? How might this situation and the feelings involved have been handled better?

Encourage your son to be an ally. Discuss strategies on how he can stand up and intervene in situations while still keeping himself safe. Could he get a group of friends to step in instead of approaching the perpetrator alone? Could he insist on getting a friend a sober or trusted driver to take them home?

Teach your son to be a critical consumer of the media and our culture at large. Point out things you notice that are misogynistic or degrading to women. Does he notice the same thing you do? How does it make him feel? Help mentor your young man on what it means to be masculine. What's good about masculinity and what parts can be harmful? How can we leave more space for a more inclusive definition of masculinity?

Talk about ways to safely party. How will your son know when he's had too much to drink? How will he keep himself and others safe when drinking? Can someone give consent if they are drunk? How does your own behavior change when you drink? How have you seen alcohol change the behavior of others when they drink?

Feminist Takeaways

While your son might still be at an age when he's trying to master the monkey bars, he's not too far off from the day when he'll be invited to attend sexist parties like "CEOs and Office Hoes." It's hard to think of your little boy growing up to be anything but the amazing man you know he can become, but it is the reality. As a parent, you are in the best position to show your son what a healthy and loving relationship looks like. Start your conversations early and often, and you'll be amazed to see the positive impact these steps make in preparing him to enter an imperfect world as a young adult.

CHAPTER 6

Use Media to Discuss Equality and Justice

We're surrounded by technology. It's hard enough to keep track of all the various cables and chargers, let alone be conscious of the messaging propagated by what's flowing through them. From the moment your son was born, you've nurtured him, sheltered him from harm, and controlled most of his environment. Losing control of our boys as they get older can be difficult—when they start receiving messages we no longer can control through friends, school, or their own phone. Parents sometimes cling so tightly to an idea of a sheltered, wholesome childhood that they truly only shelter themselves from seeing the reality that their son has already been exposed to sex, violence, misogyny, and more, through the media they consume.

In the car, Eve asked, "What's a stripper?"

Cam wondered out loud, "What is a blow job?"

And Ty has been curious about "Tossing salad."

Your jaw might be on the floor right now, and that is the general response I get when I casually talk parenting at dinner parties. But honestly—kids are exposed and learning. You can be their guardrails or not. My hunch is if this is news to you, your son has a treasure trove of questions buried in his mind that he knows you aren't comfortable with, so he just leaves them there untouched.

Never in a million years would I have expected to be talking sex with my six-year-old (just last week she asked, "Do you think you will have sex soon?"), but that is the unexpected reality of parenting. The unintended consequence is a closeness and intimacy with her. Trusted conversations we share.

"Yes, probably, Eve. Do you think you will have sex one day?"

"No. Maybe."

"You know you have to wait until you are older when your vagina is bigger so it doesn't hurt, right?"

"I know, Mom."

The conversation continued about when to have sex and why not now. I feel confident she has more education and information than the typical six-year-old, and that makes me hope she will not be one of those horrifying statistics.

Kids today more than ever are exposed to various forms of media: advertisements, games, books, television shows, movies, TikTok, YouTube, Instagram, and the list goes on. Without guidance, they're left on their own to figure out a world of misinformation and problematic representations of masculinity, identity, gender, equality, justice, sexuality, and relationships. Parents need to learn more about children's media habits, the types of media consumed, the messages they are exposed to, and how to communicate using media as a form of language their children can hear. Media is the modern currency of our boys. It's time for you to get in the game.

Access to technology today is 24/7, and when conversations aren't had at home, kids turn elsewhere. For example, porn has become the new sex ed, as the average age of first porn exposure for children is eleven years old.[124] Gone are the days of your son stashing dingy magazines under his mattress. Now it's at his fingertips in a 3-D, live, interactive, and easily accessible form— and in every variety. Misinformation and inaccurate sexual representations therefore are absorbed by our sons without discussion. And the result is that our children's view of themselves and others as sexual beings are shaped by early porn viewing.

We are parenting in a new frontier alongside technology, and the old conversations you had with your parents (if you even had them) are no longer relevant. We know that frequent media exposure shapes and impacts children's values, beliefs, dreams, and expectations.[125] At a young age, these messages shape views about gender stereotypes and cultural expectations of what it means to be a boy or girl. These become so ingrained that they influence career choices down the line, self-worth and self-esteem, and sexual and romantic expectations.

Violence is also a learned behavior. The media can perpetuate damaging beliefs regarding equality and justice when women, indigenous people, people of color, and members of the LGBTQI+ community are objectified and turned into a "thing." Portraying a person as an object rather than a human being is one of the first ways to justify violence against them.

Objectification of a person extends much deeper and more subtly than just porn, as we discussed. *Objectification* is when we reduce a person to their function or role and deny their humanity, and there are numerous examples in everyday life. We assume a woman will tidy up the kitchen after dinner. We say a polite hello to the cleaning person but then continue on with our day as if they aren't in the same room as us. We barely acknowledge the barista because all we want is our coffee, fast. You do not have to be everyone's best friend, but only seeing someone as a means to an end is how you objectify people in everyday life. Our kids are watching. Take the extra few minutes to ask questions and get to know the person behind the job. Model humanity and connection.

Oftentimes, parents think these talks should be reserved for when their son reaches high school, but by that point they've already been exposed to adult media's language and images for years. Even younger children with older siblings are hearing and seeing things that parents may not be aware of. While none of this is meant to be alarmist, it should serve as a wake-up call that we as parents need to stop sheltering ourselves from seeing the realities of the new world our children live in.

Where Is Your Son Getting Information?

LazarBeam is a popular YouTuber and "a good guy who is nice," according to Cam. But with a deeper look, I see he made a Minecraft Village out of penises. Cam laughs as he shares that he has a "specific breeding area made out of balls. He gets 'monetized' a lot." While this isn't the end of the world, it's definitely not the message I want my kid to see all day every day. Oftentimes, it is not just the media content that is sexual, it is the content that shows my kid that it is cool to stay inside and play video games all day, swear, and use impolite language. I'd rather him read a good old-fashioned book (help—I feel like a dinosaur sometimes!) and use his own imagination. But in the current culture, these YouTubers are who our kids are idealizing. The reality is, our children are being influenced by the media they consume, and as parents we need to be part of the conversation to help shape the messaging they receive.

A 2019 national survey of more than 1,600 eight- to eighteen-year-olds in the United States found that eight- to twelve-year-olds spend just shy of five hours a day consuming media.[126] That's two and a half hours watching TV or videos, one and a half hours gaming, and almost an hour on social media, browsing websites, creating content, video chatting, and/or e-reading.[127] On average, thirteen- to eighteen-year-olds spend around seven and a half hours per day on screens.[128] What messages are being delivered during this time? How much do you know of what your son is watching, hearing, or reading?

As parents, we like to believe that as long as the media consumed is "kid friendly," meaning no explicit language, violence, or sexual content, we feel we're protecting our kids from the dangers of the outside world. After all, they're just on an iPad under our roof, so how bad can it really be? It's easy to get lured into a false sense of security when we really should be considering the possible pitfalls of unsupervised access to the Internet.

In a world of a million channels, posts, clicks, and likes, there's a constant push to always up the ante. People resort to posting more and more shocking images of violence and sex because they know this will get the most attention. Or they simplify characters to one-dimensional facades whose constructed likes and dislikes are formed from generalizations or stereotypes of gender, race, and age. This limits our children's understanding of their own identities and capabilities, and takes away the opportunity for them to understand the nuance and depth of real-life individuals.

As parents, we need to help fill out these dimensions, and the first step to doing that is to acknowledge it. We can't pretend this isn't happening. We have to understand that media is a huge part of our children's lives and that we need to embrace it in order to understand and communicate in their world.

Talk About What He Knows

It's hard to accept that your son is deeply influenced by the media he consumes daily and that your eleven-year-old may already have been exposed to
sexually graphic imagery or porn. The anxiety this produces can lead even
the most level-headed parent to want to search through their son's backpack,
room, or smartphone, or interrogate him about every little detail of what he
knows. But we all know that isn't the best way to build a strong relationship
of mutual trust and honesty. Here are ways to get in the right frame of mind
to participate in his media life.

Be Unforced and Casual

There's no need for long, awkward, or drawn-out talks. Keep your conversations in manageable doses with short chats in the car or when you're
walking together somewhere. Oftentimes not making eye contact can make
the conversation easier, like when you're walking side by side, driving
together, or sitting next to one another around a fire pit. Keep your tone
casual and don't force issues he's not ready to talk about yet.

And remember, how you respond to sexuality has a direct relationship
with how your son defines and builds his own sexuality. Show him that you
can talk about these things in a casual way that lets him know this isn't a big
deal, that it's normal and just part of growing up.

Keep It Simple, Be Honest, and Stay Curious

You don't have to be an expert to be able to talk about sex, masculinity,
gender stereotypes, or other issues surrounding identity development. Just
show up with an honest curiosity about your son's world and his thoughts and
feelings. No one is asking you to have all the answers. No one wants advice
anyway. What really matters is asking good questions and actively listening
to understand. Don't approach your son with the goal of lecturing; instead be
curious.

What does he think about the world? What would he change? What are
his likes and dislikes? What views does he hold about himself and others?

What does equality and justice mean to him? Be honest with yourself and him, and don't feel pressure to know it all. If you don't know something, you can always say that and let him know you'll do some research and get back to him. He'll appreciate you sharing your own vulnerabilities and limitations with him. It shows him that everyone is grappling with these big issues in imperfect ways just like he is. Follow your son's lead and let him guide you through his world.

Empower Your Relationship and Connection

While it is natural for adolescents to become increasingly independent from their parents over time, their need for connection and meaningful relationships remains just as strong as ever. Even if it seems like your tween or teenager is trying to push you away, it's important to realize that while he does need his own space to develop, he's still looking to you for love and connection, and seeing you as a role model for what healthy relationships should look and feel like.

If you are unsure about the connection with your son, you don't know how to respond to what was said, or you don't know if it is the right moment to start a conversation around these topics, it is okay. Instead, ask yourself: *Will this interaction bring us closer together or push us farther apart? How am I prioritizing our relationship? How am I creating safety and connection in our home?* Remember, small kids have small problems, and if you can build a trusting and caring relationship when they are young, then later on, your relationship can help buffer the big problems that big kids face.

Take a Nonjudgmental Stance

Have you ever opened up to a friend about something that was hard for you to talk about, only to be judged by them and told you shouldn't feel that way? It likely felt horrible and was not productive to your healing or learning in any way. If you want to be let into your son's world, you're going to need to check your judgment at the door. This does not mean you can't set boundaries or have family values you care about. Nonjudgmental stances just help show your son that he can come to you with anything and that you will listen without having a lecture waiting at the end. By asking open-ended and non-judgmental questions, you can dive into your son's world without him redacting the parts he thinks you can't handle.

This comes up for me more often as my sons approach puberty. When with friends, I love a good sex joke. Oftentimes I am the one sharing. But when my son is talking about his erection that pops up randomly at school and I need to teach him to tuck it into his waistband, I am dying laughing on the inside but know I have to remain connected and matter of fact so as to not shame him. One day we will laugh together about this, but not today. Furthermore, send the message that masturbation is a normal part of human development. Tell your boy that he shouldn't hide the "semen sock" in his room; he can do everyone a favor by cleaning up after himself and throwing the sock in the hamper.

Here are some questions to ask to dive deeper when your son makes comments about what he's seen or heard in the media: Where did you learn that phrase? What else did you hear? What do you think it means? How does it make you feel when you hear or say it? Just remember to get curious, not furious. You will learn much more and have greater influence if you can show your son that there is nothing he can bring to you that you can't handle in a calm, collected, and nonjudgmental way.

If You Want to Know What Influences Him, Ask Him

So how much exactly does your son know about sex, relationships, equality, justice, masculinity, and his own identity? We can look up developmentally appropriate charts or speculate based on an older sibling's milestones and experiences, or we can realize none of this will actually paint a true picture. The best source of knowing what your son knows is *your son*. You might be surprised at just how much you can learn by simply showing an interest and asking questions.

Here are a few quick prompts to help get the conversation started so that you can confidently know what media your son consumes, how much, and what messages are shaping his views about himself, others, and the world around him.

- "How do you interpret what you just saw? I see XYZ, what do you see? How do you know that?" Kids might initially feel awkward or judged, but remember to be curious rather than condoning. "Huh. I notice you closed down the app when I took a peek. Is there something you want to keep private? You do not have to tell me what it is, but I wonder what makes you want to keep it to yourself?"

- "Who do you like to follow on social media and why? Can you show me some of that person's posts or videos?" Show interest and be curious.

- "Why do you think someone would write a post like this? How do you think the girl feels about whom this post is written?"

- "What do you think this song is about? What feelings does it bring up in you? Why are women depicted this way? How would you have written this song differently?"

- "I hear you singing that one song all the time, who is the artist? What is it about his music you like so much? Which YouTube channels do you find funny? Which TikTok influencers do you like? Why?"

- "What do you like to post on your own social media accounts? What do you text your friends about?"

The goal here is not to interrogate but to start casual conversations during which you can begin to gain a clearer picture of the world your son lives in, how he sees it, and the types of messages he's receiving. In my own life with two boys two years apart, who they are and how they engage with the world is quite different. They are best friends and often online, but according to Cam, "Ty watches the weird stuff on TikTok." This is true, in fact. Ty watches people doing things that, in my opinion, get categorized as "stupid shit." I find myself feeling like his IQ is actively dropping when he is online.

So I ask, "Ty, what do you like most about this video?"

He generally says something like, "It's funny."

I dig a little deeper and ask, "What makes it funny?"

Sometimes I challenge "at whose expense?" and other times I just learn. I don't always have to teach. Although I kind of hate TikTok with a passion, it is the medium in which Ty plays, so either I get acquainted or get left out.

Joint Media Engagement

We know that "unchecked media consumption of any kind is associated with greater tolerance for sexual harassment, belief in rape myths, early sexual initiation, sexual risk taking, a greater number of partners, and stereotyping of women."[129] But let's be honest. Raise your hand if you've ever felt grateful for an iPad distracting your child when you just needed a break. We're all right there with you. Technology is often designed to make our lives easier, more convenient, and efficient. I know that kids will mostly be watching media alone, and I'm not here to tell you that you don't deserve a guilt-free break. Instead, I just want to highlight some benefits of joint media engagement with your son that you can fit in here and there when you have the time.

Joint media engagement is a term coined by the LIFE Center, a collaboration between Stanford, University of Washington in Seattle, and SRI International. Joint media engagement refers to the spontaneous or intentional experience of using media with your son to learn, view, play, search, read, contribute, or create something together.[130] By sitting down and watching his favorite show with him, you're more able to engage in conversations and answer questions he might have while filtering the messages he's receiving. This engagement shows your son that you care, that you want to know about his interests, and that you're available to ask anything.

A research study developed a scale to assess parental television mediation.[131] It identified three styles of parental mediation: *restrictive mediation, social co-viewing*, and *instructive mediation*.[132]

Restrictive Mediation

Set limits and standards on what and how much media your child can access through restrictive mediation, which refers to the rules, content, and frequency of children's media consumption. Monitoring your son's media use is critical due to the ease of accessibility to content and contacts that may eclipse his emotional maturity. One way to mitigate this is by using in-app watching, like YouTube Kids, versus using an Internet browser, which makes it difficult to control the content only a click away.

For younger kids, parents sometimes choose to set limits on the amount of time a child is allowed to have access to a tablet, TV, or computer. For older kids, docking stations outside of their room in a public area can create more oversight. As your child gets older, create a list of rules with him about what appropriate Internet use for members of your family looks like.

Social Co-Viewing

Social co-viewing occurs when parents and children share in media watching together but don't necessarily engage in discussions during the viewing process. Researchers with the Children's Television Workshop (now known as Sesame Workshop) studied the effects of co-viewing and found that children learned more from the programming if their parents co-viewed with them.[133]

While it may be easy to sit next to your son on the couch and monitor and mediate what he's watching, it gets increasingly harder when he takes a tablet or laptop to his room, and even harder yet when he carries his phone everywhere he goes. Children can now use those devices in spaces that previously weren't associated with media consumption, such as the school bus, their bedroom, or the car.[134] In these situations, it's important to remember that while you may not be able to physically co-view with your child, taking an interest and making yourself available can still have a big impact.

Parental presence during computer, television, and other media use makes the chance of having conversations about their online activity as well as interpreting or evaluating comments much more likely.[135] So the next time your son is playing video games, building worlds in Minecraft, or lounging on the couch streaming a show on a tablet, take a few minutes and show some interest. Watch a bit. At the very least you'll get a better sense of the messages your son is hearing, who is giving these messages, what kind of media he enjoys engaging with, and any other factors that help shape his lived experience.

Instructive Mediation

Instructive mediation focuses on parental efforts to "ask the child questions about what he/she is viewing, to solicit the child's reactions to the content, or to model media literacy skills."[136] Instructive mediation means taking an active role in consuming media content together and building in discussions. It can be a great way to define family and individual values, discuss what they mean to your son, and talk about how the show you just watched together reinforces or veers from these values.

You can start a conversation like this: "We believe in equality for everyone. Does this show fit with this value? What makes you think that?" This doesn't need to be a long, drawn-out conversation that shuts the show down but instead can be a quick pause in programming just to get the point across that it's important to be critical consumers. This encourages your son to begin to notice differences between the outside world and his own internal and family value system. By helping guide your child through conversation during media consumption, you are helping him build his own reflective inner voice that he can fall back on when he consumes media without you.

How to Talk About Porn

Sexual development begins in utero and continues throughout the lifespan. Given how natural this process is, we don't do it well as a society. Curiosity, questioning, masturbation, and exploration are all healthy and normal parts of our developmental process. See these conversations as opportunities to show your openness (even if you're still working on it) and allow your son to see you as a trusted source for accurate information.

Whether or not you find porn to be healthy or monstrous doesn't change the fact that kids are exposed to it. Parents need to find ways to have conversations about porn instead of letting the Internet shape their child's own unchecked views of sex and sexuality. In the spirit of taking a nonjudgmental stance, let's take a quick look at why not all exposure to porn is necessarily bad.

To start, porn can help people build their sexual fantasies and learn what turns them on and off. Gay porn can be particularly helpful for gay boys who otherwise don't get much messaging around their identity and sexuality. If your child is looking at porn, ask questions about how often, for what purpose, and if it is in support of healthy relationships with his self and others. Take a curious stance to better understand the reasons behind his use and frequency, and then go from there.

Although porn can be helpful at times, it can also create unrealistic sexual expectations and depict unrealistic representations of love, intimacy, and sexual boundaries. Not all porn is equal, and some is more realistic and others are super fantasy-based. But in the absence of conversation, your son might not understand this. It is important to help him hold both. Bring home the message that sex in real life doesn't always look like this and it isn't meant to.

Pornography is void of true emotions, which are the bedrock of sexual intimacy in real life. As parents, you can engage your son in conversations about how the actors in these films are being told what to do. They have to act like they are enjoying it, whether or not they truly are. One measure of whether your son (or you) is relying too heavily on porn is whether he can only enjoy a sexual experience (alone or with someone else) with porn. Porn should be a sideshow that supports the main event.

When it comes to issues of masculinity, equality, and gender issues, help explain that pornography depicts a lot of violence against women. Men are often dominating and being aggressive toward women in degrading ways. This is a great opportunity to discuss issues of consent, physical boundaries, and respect covered in the previous chapter. Point out that pornography doesn't mention STD prevention or the use of contraceptives, which all are essential parts of making healthy decisions regarding his own body and that of his partner during sexual activities.

It can also be helpful to explain that consuming this content can result in unwarranted, negative self-worth and body image during a difficult transitionary period when his body is developing. You can help explain that porn actors' bodies are often surgically exaggerated and styled in ways that no one else actually looks like. This can help leave space for what your son expects himself and future partners to look and act like.

In the end, it's up to you as a family to decide what your views on porn are, and hopefully these conversational prompts can help prepare you for having these talks in a caring and trusting way.

Topics to Bring Up in Age-Appropriate Discussions

Now that we know just how much media is consumed by kids and how it can impact them, let's look at practical ways we can help guide our boys to foster curiosity about specific issues: masculinity and identity, equality and justice, sex and relationships. The opportunities for discussions about media consumption really come up in elementary-school years, as kids are exposed to more influences outside the home and spend more time unsupervised.

Masculinity and Identity for Kids Ages 5 to 10

- Point out moments in media when boys share their emotions in positive ways: "Did you see when the boy in the movie cried and his friend comforted him? It's okay to be sad and have these big feelings. It's so wonderful he shared them with his friend."

- Find out what he's heard about masculinity from media sources and how it makes him feel: "What is this TV show trying to tell you about being a boy? How does it make you think boys are supposed to act? What are things you like about that and what are things you don't like?"

Equality and Justice for Kids Ages 5 to 10

- Point out examples in media that give alternative ways to "do" gender: "I noticed in *Doc McStuffins* that Doc's mom works full-time to support the family and that the dad stays home to take care of the kids."

- Emphasize moments when you see media equally valuing boys and girls: "I noticed Otto and Olive in *Odd Squad* are equal partners and rely on each other to solve cases."

- Point out moments in media that focus storylines on what people do versus what they look like: "It's great to see the girls on *Project Mc²* being good at math and science, and having a TV series that doesn't just focus on their appearance."

Sex and Relationships for Kids Ages 5 to 10

- Watch movies like *Up* together and talk about the relationships he saw: "Did you notice that Carl and Ellie were a team and supported each other through all the ups and downs in life? What made them such a great team? What did you notice?"

- Point out moments in media when people in relationships are willing to compromise or admit when they are wrong: "How can people apologize and work out issues in a healthy way? What would an unhealthy response look like?"

Masculinity and Identity for Kids Ages 11 to 13

- Encourage critical thinking. When something awkward comes up in a media moment, ask open-ended questions to get your boy thinking more deeply about serious topics: "What did you hear that concerned you? What did it make you think of?"

- Call out unrealistic beauty and body standards. Compare images of men and women he sees on TV with people he knows in real life: "How are these images different? Are the standards for attractiveness the same for men and women? Why or why not? How does that make you feel?"

- When you notice non-gender-stereotyped characters, spend time discussing this with your son: "What personality traits and behaviors show us that this character rejects gender stereotypes? How does it feel to see a character who stands up against gender stereotypes? Do you think it is helpful for such characters to exist, or is it confusing?"

- Engage your son while picking out a movie to consider how our society perpetuates the idea that girls will watch "guy movies" but guys won't see "girl movies": "What is the difference between a girl movie and a guy movie? Do you agree that boys shouldn't watch girl movies? Why or why not?"

- Show examples of boys forming their own identities despite peer pressure: "What do you think about Billy Elliot's character going against what society expects of him? How do you think this shaped him or his happiness? Have you had a time you had to go against what you felt others expected of you because of your own values? How did that make you feel?"

Equality and Justice for Kids Ages 11 to 13

- Encourage your son to make observations about power dynamics between men and women: "Whose perspective is framing the story? Who has the power or the upper hand in this scene? Are the rules different for interacting with boys versus girls on social media?"

- Make observations about the way creators (filmmakers, authors, artists) represent male and female character traits, values, behaviors, and appearances: "What does this music video show about the roles of men and women? How would you describe the language used about women? Why are the women dressed that way?"

- Ask your son to consider the ratio of men to women in the media: "Can you name any strong female role models in the media? How many female characters are in this video game? How often does your character interact with a woman in a meaningful way?"

- Encourage your son to think about his own values and what changes he would make: "How do you present yourself on social media? How would you talk about the women in your life if you wrote a song? What changes would you make to represent men, women, or gender differently?"

- Help him realize the "game" of advertisements. Show him how gender, race, and appearance are all used to sell a product that can distort the way we see ourselves and others: "What are we being sold here? What do they want us to believe? What audience is this targeting and why?"

Sex and Relationships for Kids Ages 11 to 13

- Take advantage of his curiosity about sex and answer any questions to the best of your abilities. If your tween wants to explore something in more depth, help him find resources appropriate for his age.

- Offer context and perspective to the issues at hand in the news. Help your son understand unrealistic representations in media versus what real relationships look like. "I notice the girl in the TV show seems to always agree with her boyfriend and what he wants to do. That isn't how most relationships work. A healthy relationship is based on give and take, compromise, and both people having a voice. In my experience, relationships are way more interesting when people have different views and can respect others' perspectives."

- This is a great time to have conversations about pornography, the unrealistic ways it portrays relationships and sex, and gain a better understanding of your son's exposure, interest, and reactions to viewing it. "Do you ever come across pornography/sex/naked people when you are looking online? I know most kids see things, often unintentionally, and I wonder what you have seen? What was it? How did it make you feel? Do you have any questions about it? A lot of kids can be confused by what they see, and I am happy to talk about it and answer any questions."

- Have a talk about online bullying. What does that look like? How does that make someone feel? What can he do about it safely? You can say something like, "You play a lot of games online with other people who we don't know. That is great in many ways, but it can be dangerous in others. Sometimes people say mean things or do things that hurt you. These people can be friends, people you know, or strangers. Has anything like this happened to you? Or anyone you know? If it does happen, I want you to tell me. You will never be in trouble, but I can help you deal with it."

Masculinity and Identity for Kids Ages 14+

- Use moments in media to show different ways to define masculinity. In the show *This Is Us*, fathers are shown as nurturing and thoughtful. Point out moments when boys or men are expressing their emotions in constructive ways, have diverse interests, and are kind to queer characters. For example, say, "I like that guy. He says what he feels, even when it might be uncomfortable. He shows what he is feeling—I love when people do that, especially guys, because many men feel like they can't. I see it as a sign of strength."

- Make yourself available to discuss topics related to building a healthy sexual identity: "In your ideal world, how would you like others to see you in terms of relationships and sex? Would you want to be the guy who sleeps with lots of people, the guy who has a long-term relationship, or something else? There is no right answer here."

- If your son has a media hero, have conversations about what that hero's masculinity means to your son. What are his values? Who is he and who does he aspire to be? How may this differ from the way he portrays himself on social media or reacts to friends' posts? "What do you like about your favorite YouTuber? What do you think being a boy means to him? I wonder how being a boy impacts how he behaves? Do you think he ever does things because he feels like he has to as a boy? Like what? Do you think he acts differently on YouTube than he does in real life? In what way?"

- Encourage him to discuss the way social media makes him feel about himself. Talk to him about noticing when social media is harmful versus helpful. Help him manage the emotions that arise from comments from the outside world. "How do you feel after you are on social media? Do you usually feel better or worse after? How come? What do you think makes you feel that way? Do you think other kids feel that way too?"

Equality and Justice for Kids Ages 14+

- Help your teenager find his voice and see how he can make changes or address issues of gender stereotyping and inequality in his daily life. Ask him what changes he would make to a given book, film, song, or social media post to make it more inclusive and equitable. "If you had a magic wand and could make the world more equal for everyone, what would you do? Why? What could we do today or this week to try to make this better?"

- Relate the media back to his daily life and ask him if he has experienced similar stereotypes in the past. How did it make him feel? How could he respond? "It seems like _____ was judged or stereotyped for being _____. What do you think about that? Has anything like that ever happened to you?"

- Encourage him to consider the complexities of difficult subjects seen on the news, in films or books, or heard on the radio: "What forces perpetuate gender inequality? What key things would need to change for women to be paid the same as men? What could your role be now and in the future to help bring about equality in and out of the workforce?"

Sex and Relationships for Kids Ages 14+

- Point out moments in media that depict true relationships and not an idealized version. Highlight when both partners depict what it takes to build a trusting foundation. "You know, Dad and I argue sometimes when we disagree, but what I appreciate most about us, just like the couple in that show, is that we love each other and can always talk it out later, even when something really makes us mad. I know how much Dad loves me, and that is so important to me."

- Have discussions with your teen about sexting. Approach the conversation calmly and with a nonjudgmental stance. Give practical warnings about the nature of the Internet and that people online are not always who they say they are. Remind him that any pictures or messages sent can't be taken back, and that he can't always know what will be done with them on the other end. "Do you know what sexting is? It is when people send or receive sexual messages online or through text. Kids sometimes do it to be funny, or to be sexual, but it can accidentally get them into trouble. You don't know who will see the picture once you send it, you have no control over where it goes, and it can actually get you in trouble with the law. Many states have teen sexting laws that make it illegal for kids to send and receive explicit pictures."

- Keep channels of communication open and let him know he can always come to you with any questions big or small. "I know all this is confusing and I am here to help you understand."

Feminist Takeaways

In these ever-changing times, it's more important than ever to acknowl-edge the role media plays in our children's lives and learn how to commu-nicate about it. In the end, it's important to remember that "Media can be an instrument for change. It can maintain the status quo and reflect the views of the society, or it can hopefully awaken people and change minds. It just depends on who is piloting the plane."[137] So encourage your son to acknowledge what he's seeing and hearing, notice the problems it creates, and identify different ways that will create a better future for us all.

CHAPTER 7

Expand His Worldview to Cultivate Empathy

Most boys have an instinctive capacity for *empathy*, the ability to understand and share the feelings of another. Empathy is feeling, it is helping, and it is paying attention to the emotions of the marginalized. People are hardwired to empathize because we associate people who are close to us with our very selves.[138] When we get to know others, they become a part of the fabric of who we are. We actually feel what they feel. It is easy for boys to have empathy for those in their inner circle—their friend group and family. It's time to reflect on what your son's inner circle looks like. Who is in and who is out? Where is the line and why was it drawn?

It's essential to ask these questions because we need to help expand that feeling of empathy to people outside of our sons' immediate associations. He can learn to empathize with people who are different than him, who drift in and out of his awareness, and even those he will never meet.

Empathy can help us change society by helping raise emotional intelligence, improve friendships, and foster justice. When you think about the man you want your son to become, you probably picture a hardworking, dedicated person who has a great relationship with his partner and feels successful at work. Harvard Business Review recently wrote that in a recent survey of 150 CEOs, more than 80 percent stated that empathy is key to success.[139] Empathy is becoming a must-have job skill.

This chapter will help you break down a concept that we know is important but can feel big and amorphous. Developing empathy is important for your son, and it can shift the emotional tone of our culture for generations to come.

Empathy Needs to Be Developed

Though it may sound like just a good character trait, empathy is one of the most important tools for raising feminist boys and a key quality of high emotional intelligence, as you already know from chapter 3. Empathy is a learned skill that has positive benefits over a lifetime and is tied to better adjustment, better relationships, and a leg up in employment.[140] Empathy is primarily an emotional skill. It requires self-reflection and an awareness of feeling.

The distinction between empathy and sympathy is your perspective. I can feel *sympathy* for a friend grieving the loss of her mother—I feel concern for her, am moved by her situation, and want her to feel better. Or I can feel *empathy*—I can imagine what she is going through and share in her perspective. I put myself in her shoes. This is the skill we want to teach our sons.

Empathy is frequently talked about as a measurable thing that people either have a lot or a little of—and that is true—but there is more to it. Though having lots of empathy is good, what matters most is *who* we have empathy for. Someone may have a ton of empathy but only for people who look and act like themselves. This is natural and not necessarily negative, as it is easy to understand and share the feelings of people whose experiences are similar to our own.

It is also easy for boys to lose sight of their position of privilege and how it impacts their day-to-day lives. Your son might naturally empathize with a friend who got cut from the school baseball team. He can imagine how the friend feels because it is similar to experiences he has had. But your boy might have a harder time imagining why a female friend feels upset after being catcalled while on a run. Or why saying phrases like "That's gay" or "Stop being a fag" are very harmful and hurtful to others, especially those in the LGBTQI+ community. They might also have a hard time imagining why their "jokes" with friends would be offensive to different minority groups; after all, they're just kidding around, right? Wrong.

These examples illustrate how levels of empathy may vary based on how relatable the experience is to your son. As I mentioned at the beginning of this book, while our own implicit and explicit biases shape the way we see the world around us, we can work on ourselves to change these. Through self-reflection and self-awareness, we can begin to change our mental models and expand our circles of concern so that we put ourselves in other people's shoes, regardless if we share the same lived experiences or not.

How Does Empathy Relate to Feminism?

An empathic boy is the kid in the elementary school class who sits with the lonely girl at lunch, the middle school boy who stands up for the girl trying out for the football team, and the high school student who volunteers in a women's shelter. Empathy arises in our home more subtly and nuanced.

As my boys have gotten older, I feel their empathy personally focused on me. In the past few years, they have noticed when I am working a lot and taking care of them. Cam will often offer me the last piece of dessert (although I know he wants it) or Ty will (attempt) to make me lunch. Deep empathy is when he forgoes something he would want for someone else. The action and behavior is less important; the feeling behind it is what matters. They noticed someone else—me—outside of themselves, and they took action to make life just a little bit better. Because of this, it is important to notice and name his sacrifice and applaud his care.

Your son probably has no idea what it's like to be the only girl on the football team, and that's okay. What is important is that he tries to imagine what that would be like. What feelings would come up? How would he want other people to treat him if he were in that situation? It's a lot like the golden rule: treat others the way you want to be treated, but with the added component of actually imagining the other person's perspective.

The thing is, if your son has not spent much time around women or people of different ages, races, economic backgrounds, cultural perspectives, or religious beliefs, it may be difficult for him to imagine that perspective. As we talked about in chapter 3, an empathic awareness of systemic and lived experiences of marginalized groups is necessary for being a true ally. We want our sons to build this empathy as a part of their journey toward becoming feminists. Let's break down a concrete plan for building empathy at home.

Expand His Circle of Concern

Take a second and think about all the people you care about. Picture yourself at the center of a circle with different rings radiating outward. In the first ring might be your family, the second ring might contain your close friends, the third might hold your not-so-close friends, and so on. Some days, you may only care about the people in your innermost rings. Other days, your heart may feel for your community, your country, and the world at large. As an adult, you're able to flex your circle of concern based on what's going on, but that is a skill you developed over time and with practice.

Now think about your son at the center of that circle. What does his circle of concern look like? Remember, it is pretty easy for him to have empathy for the people in his innermost rings like his family, friends, and his sports team. Take a step back and think—what do the people in his circle *literally* look like? Are they all the same? Are all the friends in his inner circle male? Notice this, judgement-free.

Expand His Circle Through New Experiences

If your son interacts with the same people over and over again, those are naturally the people he will care about and be able to empathize with. Though this isn't bad or wrong, you can broaden this instinctive empathy by helping him expand his world. By having more diverse friends in his inner circle, his empathy toward others will naturally increase.

Take a look around. How many boys are in dance classes? How about in art activities or in drama club? Encourage your son to try non-gendered or stereotypically female hobbies. He may find out he loves art class or gymnastics, and these activities may expose him to female voices and different ways of playing and being. My sons love cooking. We research recipes, shop, and cook together for hours. Not only do they participate in an activity that might be defined as historically more feminine, they appreciate the effort, time, and cost cooking for others takes. It helps build empathy.

Here are some ideas for expanding his circle of concern through new experiences:

- Form new, coed playgroups that introduce him to girls as friends, not as girlfriends or love interests.

- Consider sports neutrally. Sports are not a required activity for boys. They can be wonderful tools for teaching teamwork, communication, and problem-solving. They are also a fun way for kids to stay active, exercise, and make friends. That being said, if your son dislikes sports for valid reasons, consider other options and directly offer them.

- Encourage your son to take part in non-gendered activities like kayaking, cross-country running, skiing, surfing, or rock climbing. He can also try out being in non-gendered spaces like the great outdoors. Spending time in nature can be a wonderful way for both boys and girls to explore together. Participating in coed activities exposes your son to new types of people and ways of being that don't involve typically masculine characteristics, such as rough-and-tumble play.

Get Him to Notice Those Outside His Circle

Sometimes a byproduct of privilege, or the unearned access to resources, is a lack of awareness of those outside of that privilege. Teach your son to be aware of people who may be outside his social circle or his own category of privilege (think back to the privilege assessment in chapter 4). Here are some suggestions for guiding conversations around noticing:

- Ask him about kids at school that he *doesn't* hang out with or who seem lonely. "Who is often by themselves? Who in your class seems like they need a friend?"

- If your son is excited about getting his driver's license and car for his sixteenth birthday, ask him to pause and think about the privilege that represents. Who isn't able to get a car? How would not being able to drive affect someone's life?

- Have him list his closest friends, and then ask him how he'd feel about adding new people into his friend circle? Why or why wouldn't he want to add someone? What are the criteria he would base this decision on? Who is being left out of the group?

Zoom In and Out

Harvard's Making Caring Common Initiative suggests that you teach children to zoom in and zoom out.[141] This means teaching your son that there are times when it is appropriate to tune in to one person, and there are also times to take in multiple perspectives and people. Zooming in and zooming out is fluid and can change with time based on having your son pay attention to his own internal compass and assessing when he needs to be available to his friend versus tackling a larger-scale issue.

Your son may have times in his life when he needs to focus on supporting one friend and times when he can volunteer at a local organization and focus on more systemic issues affecting the community at large. There is no right or wrong answer here, but just being curious and getting this idea on his radar helps build empathy and awareness of self and other.

- Encourage your son to put down screens and engage in conversations with family and friends fully, especially when they need support and encouragement.

- Encourage your boy to discuss social issues with others.

- As a family, decide to do something together to support others, like working a soup kitchen, getting groceries for the elderly, or saving up a portion of allowances to donate together.

- Help your son learn to take stock of the emotional temperature of himself, his friends, and the group. When he can accurately assess, he'll better gauge when he needs to zoom in versus zoom out, that is, spending time with a friend one on one versus being in a group setting.

- Persuade him to write a Letter to the Editor of a news site to share his opinion on larger issues he cares about.

- Inspire him to run for student council to help get his fellow students' voices heard.

Talk Openly and Honestly When Discomfort Arises

When your boy is exposed to people who are different than himself, he may have questions that make you feel embarrassed or awkward: "Why does he look like that?" "Why does she use crutches?" "Why do they wear those weird outfits?"

These are natural reactions to differences and are a great time for you, as a parent, to model empathy. Just this morning, my kid said, "Ty told Eve that she looks like her" and pointed to an overweight, potentially disabled Black woman on TikTok. My first inclination was to say, "That is not nice" (which I did), and then I expanded to say, "How do you think that woman feels being used as a criticism? How would you feel if that were you?"

I tried to remain nonjudgmental and curious, rather than punishing, but it is these small, everyday moments when our children need to be challenged. Don't shut down these questions, as curiosity is valid and understandable. Use his curiosity as an opportunity to explain that differences are normal and to link to the emotional experience of the person on the other side, even if they aren't here.

Embrace "We-ness"

Think "we" not "me." "We-ness" is not the most American concept. We're accustomed to a culture in which people prioritize themselves and value independence and autonomy. This can make empathy difficult. In fact, a University of Michigan study found that college students in the United States today are about 40 percent lower in empathy than they were thirty years ago.[142] The United States has a "me" problem. As parents, it is our role to break this cycle. By raising more empathetic sons, we can help create a new generation of men who embrace the "we."

Try Hygge

Hygge (pronounced "hoo-gah") is a Danish term that best translates to "cozy togetherness." Hygge is a time of coziness with family and friends and, most important, it revolves around togetherness. When I think of *hygge*, I picture my family playing board games in front of a nice fire with everyone in pajamas and soft music playing in the background. No screens and no drama. While this sounds amazing, it isn't realistic all of the time, just something to aim for.

Try setting aside a time to create an accepting, cozy, emotionally nourishing safe space. Here are some *hygge* suggestions that have been modified from Jessica Joelle-Alexander's "Hygge Oath" in *The Danish Way of Parenting*:[143]

- Turn off phones and other handheld devices.

- Leave drama at the door.

- Don't complain unnecessarily.

- Look for when we can help out, so that no one person gets stuck doing all the work.

- Light candles if inside.

- Make a conscious effort to enjoy food and drinks.

- Do not bring up controversial topics like politics; those discussions can happen at other times.

- Tell and retell funny, lovely, and uplifting stories about each other from the past.

- Don't brag too much; bragging can be subtly divisive.

- Don't compete; think "we" not "me."

- Don't talk bad about others or focus on negativity.

- Play games.

- Make a conscious effort to feel gratitude for the people around us who love us.

Use "We" Language

Prioritize *collectivist thinking* and listening—that means prioritizing "we" over "me." Think about what works best for the group, not for the individual. As a parent, name that you are doing this and explicitly teach your son how it feels better for everyone when we do this. The easiest place to start is within your own family unit. By talking about and viewing yourselves as a unified group, you create a feeling of love, inclusion, and belonging. People are their best selves when they feel this way.

Here are some strategies for using "we" thinking within your family:

- Consider: If I say this, will it move the group forward or backward? Vocalize this mindset to your son. If your son says something unkind to a family member, ask him what impact he thinks that has on the family unit.

- Make household tasks joint responsibilities that everyone benefits from and contributes to: "We are cooking dinner as a family tonight. It would help all of us if you could do your part and set the table."

- Ask and get feedback on family activities: "What activities can we do together that we all will enjoy?"

Emphasize the "we" in being on a team: If your son enjoys sports or any game-based activity, you've likely heard the after-a-loss blame game (for example, "We would have won if [insert name here] hadn't messed up at the end!"). If you hear this type of singling out, bring him back to the "we" by reminding him of the team's collective action. This may sound like, "The game is the result of everyone's actions. You can focus on one action, but there are tons of little things each person contributed or didn't contribute. You guys are all working together toward the same goal."

Expanding his circle of concern means that "we" doesn't have to look like "me." Find places where your son is included in a diverse group and builds a sense of we-ness with people who are different from himself. This may bring up uncomfortable feelings for him and may take some getting used to. Recently, my own son began playing on a coed soccer team. He said something along the lines of "Sarah can't be on my team because she's a girl!"

This is a fairly common reaction—society has taught my son, and yours, that for whatever reason boys and girls need to play on different teams. It is our job, as parents, to help our kids unlearn this divisiveness.

Show your boy examples of female excellence. As soon as I showed my son videos of the USA women's soccer team led by Megan Rapinoe, he didn't have any qualms about a girl playing on his team. Point out to him that having excellent women in his group only elevates performance for everyone. Ask some deeper questions:

- "Why do you not want a girl on your team/in your play group/as a project partner?"

- "Do you really think it will be weird?"

- "What can you do to make her feel included?"

Model Empathy

As parents, you are your child's first role model and best example. Like it or not, he looks to you for guidance on how to think, look, act, and behave, and he is pretty much always listening. Try these strategies for modeling empathy:

Display Equal Empathy for All Genders

Kids internalize and reflect back the behaviors that are directed toward them. If parents treat boys with less empathy, they will internalize that they are supposed to suppress feelings in favor of being stoic and tough.

An Emory University study found that fathers of daughters were more attentively engaged, sang more, and used more language to acknowledge sadness. In contrast, fathers of sons engaged in more rough-and-tumble play and used more achievement language like "win" and "proud."[144]

Knowing that parenting behaviors differ based on a child's gender, let's reflect on how you respond when a female versus a male is crying. Traditionally, crying from a female will prompt an adult or peer to comfort her through words or reassuring touches. On the other hand, a male may be told to suck it up or get over it. Our culture has repeatedly shut down displays of emotion from men, but this also shuts down how they may respond to displays of emotions from others.

Avoid saying things like, "You are okay," when your son is crying and you don't actually know if he is okay yet. Follow his emotional cues, which might mean just giving a silent hug until he tells you what he needs. Or just ask what he needs when he settles.

Teach your boy to embrace his own feelings so that he can validate and support the feelings of others. Emotionally support your boy and be conscious of stereotypes that view him as overly tough or strong. He needs empathy from you too!

Validate and Name His Emotions

Other times when our boys are upset or angry, we just want to fix it right away. Because we have developed empathy as parents and our sons are a part of the fabric of our being, it hurts us to see them in pain (or it can just be loud and annoying). We give them the popsicle or the iPhone in the hopes that it will stop the wailing or grouchiness. Experiencing unpleasant emotions, however, is a part of life they need to learn to handle.

Next time stuff goes haywire, try naming the emotion and accepting it as valid. "I know you really wanted five more minutes of screen time, so I understand that you are feeling sad. It's so hard to have to put the iPad away." This validates his feelings and models language that he can use when others are experiencing difficult feelings.

Talk About Other People's Feelings

Talking about other people's feelings gives your son a low-stakes way to practice using empathy. It may feel a little weird at first, but this can be helpful for your son at any age. For younger boys, you can start with book or television characters. You can discuss how the characters may be feeling or ask simple questions such as, "Does she look happy or sad? What do you think she is feeling? How would you feel if…?"

As your son ages, the nature of the conversation can remain the same, just at a higher level. "Wow, your friend is going through a really difficult time right now. He must be feeling so overwhelmed." Talking about other people's feelings requires your son to reflect and try a different perspective. It ultimately normalizes feelings by discussing them openly.

Do Acts of Service for Others

Every fall, my family fundraises and participates in the Best Buddies Friendship Walk. This is my favorite family act of service, as it is personally connected to us (my sister had disabilities and my niece has Down syndrome). We ask friends and family to donate, create T-shirts, and ultimately do the walk together. It was the first 5K all of my kids ran. I share that not for accolades but for how good it felt as a family to do something for someone else—for people we are not connected to but care about. The feeling is visceral, the event is upbeat and energizing, and it helps connect my kids to the feel-good feeling of stepping beyond ourselves.

Whether your son realizes it or not, you do a lot for other people, both within your family and in your larger community. An easy way to foster compassion for others is to invite him into this service, whether it's through volunteering in the community or supporting each other within the home.

For instance, if a member of your family has a bad day or is struggling with a difficult emotion, ask your son, "What are some ways we could make your sister/brother/dad feel better?" "If you were having a bad day, what do you think you would need or want?" Encourage him to brainstorm ways to support his family member with compassion and empathy.

Bring your son to community service events. Your local church, food bank, shelter, or school likely needs volunteers throughout the year. Your boy will enjoy spending time with you in service of his local community while also providing you with opportunities to lead deep conversations about empathy and compassion. You can pose questions like, "What do you think it would be like to not be able to get enough to eat?" "Why is it important that we support other people in our community?"

When your son acts in a caring way, stop for a moment and acknowledge his actions. Let him know what you see and what you appreciate. As parents, we're often quick to praise our sons for their grades and accomplishments but then let moments of kindness go unnoticed. Instead, praise your son's acts of kindness and help him build positive experiences around empathy and compassion. If he sees that you notice and value these efforts, it will help him to build his own value system around empathy, compassion, and acts of service for others as well.

Show and Share Your Own Emotions

This is a tricky one. For so many of us, we were taught from a young age to suppress and subdue our own emotions. Mothers, especially, are often messaged by society to be selfless and push aside their own emotions to be strong for their children. Mothers oftentimes feel they need to protect their children from the emotions they experience themselves. While this may be appropriate at times, kids are naturally excellent sensors of the emotional mood at home. They pick up on the feelings in the environment, and if they are at an appropriate developmental stage your change in mood can be an opportunity to have honest discussions about your own feelings, model effective coping strategies, and encourage your child to employ empathy appropriately.

Here are some guiding questions and statements to navigate conversations about your own feelings:

- Start conversations by naming your feeling: "I am feeling _____."

- Explain the emotion: "I am feeling this way because _____."

- Name what you need: "It would be helpful for me if you _____."

- Or maybe there is nothing your son can do. That's okay too. Just try and explain the best you can: "There is nothing you can do for me right now. I just need time/space/a hug."

- Thank him for his empathy: "I really appreciate you checking in on me. That is so thoughtful."

- Remember to talk about positive emotions too! It's easy to reserve conversations about your own emotions for when you are visibly upset or distressed, but the opposite is crucial too. Talk to your child about your feelings of happiness, joy, or excitement.

Empathy Building Strategies by Age

It is never too young to start teaching empathy. As you already know, empathy is a core component of high emotional intelligence, and helping your son foster this skill early on only promotes his emotional intelligence.

Skills for Kids Ages 0 to 4

When children are little, it is normal for them to be focused on themselves. They aren't mean, they are developmentally normal. That said, helping boys start to notice their own and other people's feelings and thoughts is a fantastic starting point.

- Teach emotional language and pair it with his emotion: "I see you stomping your feet and yelling—it looks like you're mad."

- Use an emotion chart to help your boy label basic emotions. Having the language cuts down on a lot of frustration.

- Empathize and validate all emotional experience. Help him feel okay expressing his emotion. Remember, all emotion is okay—all behavior is not.

- Plant the seed of empathy through trying to imagine what someone else might feel in the moment: "I saw Teddy playing alone in the corner of your preschool classroom. Have you ever done that before? How did you feel? What do you think Teddy was feeling in that moment? How do you know?"

Skills for Kids Ages 5 to 10

Your son is receiving messages from the world every day about the way he and others act, dress, and behave. Some of those messages may need to be counteracted. Here are some specific tips to make sure that your son is developing his empathy and emotional intelligence:

- Talk about his feelings, learn to label them, and find strategies to help him calm himself when he feels overcome by them.

- Make empathy a priority when talking about your son with others, and ask other adults about your child's positive social relationships. In your next parent-teacher conference, try asking the teacher if your son is a compassionate classmate. Ask his coaches if he's a good teammate. This shows your son and the adults in his life that positive prosocial behavior is just as important as his achievements.

- Talk to your child about gender in the classroom. Ask about friendships he has formed with the people of other genders, and remember not to frame these relationships as romantic. Use guiding questions: "Are students often separated by gender for activities? Does your teacher call on girls and boys the same amount? Which are your friends who are girls? What is fun about spending time with them?"

- Encourage empathy through play. Through acting out different characters, kids practice perspective taking and empathy. Why not try activities like "Playing House" or playing with dolls? Encourage boys to literally assume other identities. Role-play is an excellent activity in empathy, but society has pretty much told boys that this type of play is only for girls. Show him that that perspective is just not true.

- Practice strategies for resolving conflicts. Role-play is a great tool here, as is experience. If your son has a conflict with a peer, refrain from disciplining him automatically. Instead, ask probing questions to understand the situation and encourage him to think from a different perspective.

- Teach him to notice and look out for others. Your son may be super kind and sweet, but also a little oblivious. Young boys can be incredibly focused on their own problems and goals, sometimes at the expense of not noticing other people. Try some of these questions: "Who do you think is the loneliest one in your class? Who doesn't have people to play with? How would you feel if no one wanted to play with you?"

Skills for Kids Ages 11 to 13

Boys in middle school are exploring their own identity and how that identity relates to others, including sexual attraction. This is a particularly ripe time for cultivating empathy.

- Take a curious stance about his classmates and friends. Ask genuine, but not gossipy, questions about how his peers are doing. By taking an inquiring stance, you model thoughtfulness about other people's lives. You can demonstrate ways to celebrate others' successes or help out through their hardships.

- Encourage friendships with people of different sexes, and be sure not to romanticize these relationships. He may be involved in short-lived romances involving texting, conversations, and hanging out. Though it may not look like real "dating," this is a great time to engage in conversations about the role of empathy in relationships.

- Keep talking about and validating emotions. Remember, you can validate the emotion without liking the behavior. Here are some go-to validation and reflection phrases: "I see you are sad/happy/angry. It is so normal that you feel that way."

- Talk to your son about media. Though you don't have control over all the media your son consumes, especially in the age of smartphones, think about the books he's reading, the shows he's watching, and the games he's playing. How can you increase his exposure to content with female protagonists through media? If you notice that your son only consumes media that features male leads, talk about it with him from a curious, judgment-free perspective.

- Unfortunately, as our children develop into tweens, bullying begins to increase. Ask your child if bullying is occurring at school. If so, frame an empathetic conversation around how both the bully and bullied children feel: "How do you think they feel? How would you feel if it were you? What can you do to help? How can you do this in a way that keeps you and others safe?"

- Discuss real-world examples. The news is full of difficult and confusing information. You don't need to bombard your son with sad stories, but as things come up ensure that he is processing things in a thoughtful way. Point out awesome examples of empathy as you see them.

Skills for Kids Ages 14+

By this point, your son has most likely already developed empathy. High schoolers can put empathy to work by moving from being passive perspective takers to being active advocates.

- If you haven't already, be clear about your expectations. Be sure he knows that there is a strong ethical obligation to treat all with kindness and respect.

- Shift the conversation from passivity to action. Tell him that standing up for what is right is an important part of being an ally in difficult situations. Bystanders who witness atrocious acts can have empathy, but it matters little if they stand by and watch.

- Help your high schooler understand that the world does not revolve around him. His feelings are valid, but sometimes concern for others should outweigh his own happiness.

- Encourage him to volunteer in the local community.

Feminist Takeaways

Building empathy is an ongoing, lifelong process, and it begins with how you, as a parent, cultivate it. Because empathy produces the courage to do the right thing. And it's a key ingredient in social change: feminist boys are empathic. And those empathic boys will grow up to be our future men. As a parent, you have so much power to make things better for your son. Start now. Download the Oath of Respect, Equity, and Empathy at http://www.newharbinger.com/46677 and talk with your son about what this means for your family. By giving him the skill of empathy, you teach him to relate more deeply to you, his family, his community, and his world.

CHAPTER 8

Repair Relationships When Harm Is Done

When we're learning new things, mess-ups are inevitable. They don't make you a bad person. You are human. It would be fantastic if sexism, racism, homophobia, ageism, ableism, and every form of discrimination weren't a thing and all people could walk this world safely and be treated equally and fairly. Unfortunately, that's not reality—yet.

The truth is, we all are a part of an unequal system and its biases. We need to notice and acknowledge our part in it to bring about meaningful and lasting change. This book has given you the tools you need on this journey to become a change agent. Along the way, it is inevitable that you'll "mess up" at some point by saying something, doing something, or not saying or doing something. These are called *microaggressions*, and we'll take a look at these more closely together. In chapter 1, you explored your implicit and explicit biases, and in this chapter we'll look at how these arise in language and behavior. Know that they exist and plan for what to do when they surface, both within yourself and in front of others.

We aren't aiming for perfection. We are aiming for self-awareness, responsibility, and some form of action. Essentially, when you realize you've messed up, notice it, name it, and say or do something different.

Mess-Ups Are Microaggressions

Explicit bias, sexism, racism, and more blatant "-isms" are easier to spot and respond to. What is harder to work with are the everyday and often subtle put-downs targeted at marginalized groups. Unfortunately, these microaggressions are commonplace and come part and parcel with implicit bias, which unconsciously steers our decisions, actions, and understanding of those around us.

Unfortunately, when left unchecked, we may carry implicit biases about people from different races, ethnicities, or cultures that make us cause harm without necessarily realizing the impact of our words, actions, thoughts, or feelings. Microaggressions happen all the time and can glide past our awareness, especially when you are not part of the marginalized group. What do microaggressions against women look like?

Any assumption based on gender is a microaggression, like saying to a guy, "You must not know how to cook," or to a girl, "Wow, that is impressive! You skate great!" implying that it is unexpected that the girl on the hockey team is talented.

A microaggression can take the form of "mansplaining"—when a man explains something to a woman in a condescending way because she is a woman. An example of this can be a man trying to tell a woman how she should feel about childbirth because he read an article somewhere about it, all the while completely disregarding her own *actual* lived experience.

Another example was when a little eight-year-old boy I know told his teammates that he saw the girl on his team "naked" in the hockey locker room. He thought he was being silly, but when the rumor got around to his female teammate (and her parents), it became quite clear it was not funny and was completely humiliating for her. Although the little boy did not intend to target his female teammate, she was the target of his joke because she was female. This exemplifies not only implicit bias but also a microaggression.

An adult example is when a potential new hire interviews for a job and a male employee says, "Let's hire her—she's easy on the eyes." Although that man might have believed his remarks were harmless and potentially even complimentary, it sent the message that women are to be objectified. Although the interviewee was not there, it sent the message to everyone else that judging women's physique is tolerable, acceptable, and more important than her professional qualifications.

Among friends, someone might say something like "I'd love to bang _____" as an outrageous throwback to our old high school vibe. Instead of laughing along, now I am more inclined to say, "You know you sound like a middle-age asshole, don't you?" The way I think about it is this: if I am in the cut-throat dude vibe where comments like that are allowed, it is also allowed for me to give it right back in the same tone.

Imagine you find yourself debating a recent news piece on a woman at a college club who drank too much, was dancing provocatively on the bar, and was sexually assaulted later that night. You engage in the debate with your friend about whether she caused the sexual assault. That is a microaggression. Did you catch it? No behavior *causes* sexual assault. No matter what a victim is doing, a rapist is responsible for raping her. Nobody deserves to get raped, and the only person responsible is the rapist.

There are common gender-based microaggressions that are unfortunately still commonplace in our culture. Here is a list of a few of them to help you better see the bias and name it.

- Objectifying people: "I can see why you like having Emma as a lab partner. She's hot."

- Treating other genders like second-class citizens by talking down or not including them: "Dads do not parent as well as moms."

- Use of sexist language: fireman, stewardess, male nurse, and so on. Instead say firefighter, flight attendant, nurse.

- Assuming someone does not know something based on their gender: explaining to a girl how to fix a flat tire without considering she might already know how.

- Expecting someone to do something based on their gender: asking your daughter, "Can you do the laundry?" and your son, "Can you take out the trash?"

- Limiting people based on their gender: "Let your brother do that— he is stronger!"

- Denial of sexism as "a thing": "Sexism was a thing of the seventies, but it's the twenty-first century now and I don't see it."

- Invalidation of another gender's lived experience: "Are you sure that you are reading the situation right? Pete is a great guy and really likes girls."

- Ignoring someone based on their gender: "I can't invite that stay-at-home dad for coffee and a playdate. He's going to think I'm into him."

- Jokes based on gender: "How many blondes does it take to…"

- Systemic issues like lower wages, glass ceilings, and all-male boards or sports coaches: "I'd really like to have a woman on the board, but I haven't been able to find anyone who is a woman and is qualified."

Unfortunately, moments like these happen all too often for women. Other oppressed and marginalized people also experience these forms of making assumptions, dismissing their realities, being the brunt of "harmless" jokes that actually hurt deeply, and having physical appearance override qualifications.

As a parent focused on raising a feminist boy, be a microaggression detective. When you start paying attention, they pop up everywhere. I push myself to say something, although my natural inclination is to let the moment pass.

When I am in a place that is less comfortable (like a professional environment), I use nonverbal communication a lot. A phrase that often is still more widely used than I would imagine is "she is crazy." When someone uses that word as an insult, I make a "yikes" face and the person usually says, "What?" Humor is my go-to approach, and I will say something like, "You know it's not 1992 anymore, right? You can't say stuff like that anymore." Humor is built into my natural dialogue, so it's not a long shot to use it to deal with microaggressions. If they ask more, I'll say, "Saying a woman is crazy reinforces a gender stereotype. What does that actually mean? What are you actually tying to say?" In general, I think the approach is to assess:

1. Is it worth saying something?

2. If yes, is it worth saying something in the moment or later?

3. If yes, what approach? *Humor* ("You know you sound like a dinosaur when you say stuff like that?") or *straight honesty* ("Your intention may be good, but when you said _____, it made me a little uncomfortable because that is offensive because _____. I bring it up because I care about you and our work culture, and I know you do too. We all are learning about this stuff as we go.")

What to Do When You Mess Up

Have you ever said something along the lines of "Be careful with Erica. She isn't used to playing with you guys and I don't want her to get hurt"? Or "Madison is gorgeous. I bet all the boys are in love with her"? These are microaggressions that gender someone and their behavior in one way or another.

Because we are culturally ingrained, these types of comments can easily slip off the tongue. Among longtime friends with whom I am really comfortable, it's easy to default to old, dated, and sexist language. I have to catch myself from saying that so and so "is such a bitch." Although I am pretty sure most of my friends would not bat an eye, I make an effort to notice and name it. Calling a fellow woman a bitch reinforces sexism by dividing women and using language that the sexist culture has used against women. It is a form of internalized oppression, which means the oppressed group uses the language that the dominant group has used against them. If I slip up, I might say, "Ugh. Uncool. I didn't mean 'bitch.' I meant 'asshole' because…" I know, I am not being nice, but if I am going to not be nice, at least I am not going to be sexist too.

Because we are culturally ingrained, these types of comments can easily slip off the tongue.

Here's what to do if you notice you made a microaggression:

1. Stop.

2. Notice what you said.

3. Reflect on why it was gendered or sexist.

4. Name it out loud.

5. Offer another solution such as, "It would have been better if I said _____."

6. Ask the other person how they're feeling.

7. Vow to learn from the moment and then move on.

Some alternative messages you can use to correct yourself include, "Guys, Erica wants to play. Erica, let them know if anything is unclear." Here, you are not making assumptions about Erica's fragility or strength. Instead, you are including her, and you give her the power to ask for what she needs.

Generally, stay away from making comments about people's physical looks. It emphasizes the wrong focus and sends the message that looks matter most. As a matter of principle, try to stay clear and focus on the function of how the body works, rather than form. For example, "Madison is so strong. She is a top athlete at the middle school."

Requesting that female teens or tweens babysit is part of a culture that has taught us women are better caretakers. This is problematic for a number of reasons. It puts the burden on women, it excludes men, and it sends the message to your sons that taking care of each other is gendered. Assume everyone has equal ability to caretake.

What to Do When Your Son Messes Up

Your son is human too, and it is inevitable that he will do or say things that are outside of your realm of acceptance. It might look like this: on a group text chain, he calls a girl "a bitch." Or he looks the other way when his friends make a mean comment about a gay kid. Or he isn't particularly warm to the boy on his team who isn't as "jocky" as he is.

First off, start by having some compassion. Use moments like these not to shame or judge but to teach. Normalize the discomfort he feels and ask him to pay attention to it. You can ask, "What is your body telling you?" "How are you reacting emotionally?" "Why do you think you responded that way?"

Then you can explore alternative ways of responding by honoring his discomfort while encouraging new behaviors. You can follow up with: "What made it hard to speak up?" "What would you have wanted to say if you could do it again?" "How could you say that in a way that is true to your feelings and also respectful of the other person?"

This will help your boy think ahead about how to be an upstander and plan for it. An *upstander* is someone who sees something that isn't right and speaks up or does something about it. Being an upstander takes courage and can feel difficult, but this role has long-term gains like positive self-esteem, a sense of pride, and respect from others who witnessed his courage.

A *bystander*, on the other hand, is someone who sees an injustice happening but doesn't say anything. Although this might be the easiest response in the moment, it doesn't feel good, others might see you as weak, and it is generally unkind. Inspire your son to be an upstander by encouraging him to:

- Not join in or laugh along.

- Support the person of focus publicly—tell friends they aren't being cool and are just being mean.

- Support the person of focus privately: "I am sorry they said or did that to you. That must not have felt good. How are you? Is there a way I can help?"

- Use the power of the social structure—join with other friends to speak up.

- Talk to an adult. There is a difference between *tattling* (the goal is to get someone in trouble) and *getting help* (the goal is to get someone out of trouble, whether physical or emotional).

Feminism, Equality, and Justice Take Ongoing Work

If building an equitable community was simple, it would have already been accomplished. While this doesn't mean challenging the status quo is impossible, it does require ongoing awareness and action. These are ways to approach the ongoing work of feminism.

Repair Any Hurts

Think of when an important person missed your birthday, remembered a few days later, made light of it, and hoped to just move on. That is an unprocessed *rupture,* or the "issue" that caused a break in the relationship. Yes, of course, you can move on, but very little was learned from the experience and a lingering resentment or pain can remain.

A rupture that is followed by a *repair*—an act of healing when the rupture is acknowledged, named, and taken responsibility for—actually deepens the relationship and brings people closer than before the rupture. Imagine if this same person forgot your birthday, remembered at some point, and not only apologized but also acknowledged the impact of their forgetting by saying something like, "I'm so sorry I missed your birthday. You're so important to me. How was it for you that I forgot?" You would be free to say, "Yes, it was hard. You're important to me too, and I was curious if something had happened between us." Notice how this type of dialogue brings more intimacy and connection rather than disconnection.

Another example is not standing up for a woman at work who is being mansplained to. There are different ways to handle it. You can go back to the person mansplaining and let him know what he was doing, or go directly to the woman and acknowledge your part in it as a bystander. Acknowledge, name, and take responsibility—all important parts of repairing the rupture.

Let's bring this idea to gender equity. Say your son finds himself hanging out with guy friends. He gets swept into the culture of masculinity and calls his friend "a girl" when he shares a time when he was scared. Yes, it seems harmless, but he is in fact calling his friend a derogatory word for a woman and implying he is less than. That is a microaggression. A feminist boy could follow up that moment by thinking about the harm he caused and finding ways to correct them. He might approach his friend later and say, "Hey, I'm sorry about calling you a girl. I actually think girls are really great and didn't mean to drag them down in the process. I wasn't really thinking. I'm sorry."

These moments pop up all over the place. Have your son notice them, name them, and say something different. "Oops, that wasn't cool. I just called you a girl" or "I'm sorry I just told you to 'suck it up like a man' when you were being really vulnerable with me. I think that came from me just being uncomfortable talking about emotions, and that's something I definitely want to work on. I hope you know you can come to me and maybe you can help me work on this. Sorry again!"

Here's an example from my own life. Eve, as my third child, has always tried to keep up with her brothers. And she generally does. She's tough as nails, rides dirt bikes, wrestles like the best of them, and can bounce back from scrapes and bruises like no other. When my son called out to his sister and told her flat out she was a tomboy, I wanted to say, "Yes, Eve is a tomboy and does whatever the fuck she wants!"

You see, I was considered a "tomboy" too growing up. Something inside of me at that moment just wanted to show him that Eve was just like me and that being a tomboy was awesome and cool. And while that was the first thought that came to mind, when I took a moment to reflect, I recalled that I don't want to gender behaviors that are inherently ungendered. What I actually said to my son was that Eve is not a tomboy or a boy at all. She is herself. She is a girl who likes dirt bikes, wrestling, winning, and getting dirty. She also likes to play house and cook and cuddle puppies. She is Eve. She is cool. And she is all girl.

Moments of repair not only feel better for the people involved, they also punch a hole in the fabric of sexist dialogue. It sends the message that you care enough to say something different. That allows others who may feel marginalized, discriminated, or otherwise hurt to speak up to you, your coworkers, your friends, and most important, your son.

Read

Read a variety of books to your son from a young age to help him understand others' experiences. We are in a very ethnocentric world, so explore other narratives. Gender is experienced differently depending on a person's race, class, language, ability level, or religion. For lists of books about gender and sexual identity by age, as well as for a selection of titles by authors of color, see the Suggested Reading List online at http://www.newharbinger. com/46677.

Listen and Talk

Listening and talking about a topic can feel heated before it even begins. Set yourself up for the best outcome by going into every conversation assuming the best intention of the other, and ask that they do the same of you. Commit (together) to pushing through the discomfort. This will help strengthen your relationships by helping you refine your skills of active listening, empathy, perspective taking, reflective thinking, emotional validation, and conflict resolution.

Imagine a world where everyone employed these skills to come to the table and talk about their emotions, thoughts, struggles, fears, and hopes. A place of honesty, trust, and authenticity is a place we all would want to be.

Learn

Join reading groups, attend lectures, step outside of your usual routine, and commit to learning about feminism, racial inequalities, and other issues facing oppressed and marginalized communities. Talk to someone new in your community and learn about their experiences as an "outsider" coming into a new group, town, or school. What can you do to make their transition easier?

Watch a documentary with some friends or your family about gender, sexism, race, or discrimination, and plan to have a conversation afterward about it together. Leave room for *all* opinions and views, and practice active listening and a nonjudgmental spirit of curiosity.

Connect with Others

You can say all the right things, but if your boy doesn't actually *see* you seeking a diverse community, he knows it's just lip service. Look for ways to expand your community to include all genders and diversity in all forms. Remember, feminism is about equality for everyone. So work to create a community that reflects everyone.

Expand your friend circle and that of your son's to include people outside of your habitual groups. There's so much we can learn from others with different lived experiences. Our world is diverse and beautiful, so embrace it by being open to change and getting out of your set ways, routines, and usual circles.

Feminist Takeaways

Once you start looking, you can find microaggressions everywhere. It is difficult to see them made by people you know and don't know, and even yourself. Fortunately, now you have a road map for what to look for, how to respond, and what to do to avoid making microaggressions yourself.

The truth is, we live in a flawed world and we ourselves are also flawed. We all make mistakes, say things we wished we hadn't said, and do things we wish we hadn't—and all of that makes us human. Dwelling on the past won't change the future—but learning from it will. What matters is that you are reading this book. Engaging in dialogue. Reflecting on your own biases. Aspiring to be and do better. No one is asking for perfection. Take one step at a time. Reflect. Ask questions. Be curious.

Moving Feminism Forward

Now that you've reached the end of this book, take a moment to reflect on your own journey and applaud yourself for endeavoring to raise a feminist son. The topics in this book have ranged from building empathy and attachment, to how to talk about porn with your child and normalize bodily changes, to how to address microaggressions and implicit and explicit biases and privilege. I know these topics aren't easy to sort out on your own, and that's why I have created a Group Reading Guide available for free at this book's website, http://www.newharbinger.com/46677. Be sure to check out the Suggested Reading List and other bonus material there as well.

Those are the concrete tools we have covered. The thing is, this endeavor goes well beyond a how-to book for me, and I imagine for you too. I didn't write this and you didn't read this because we want to be perfect parents. Gawd knows that is not happening, and we are all just doing the best we can to raise kind, happy boys. Boys who have enough self-awareness and security to not hurt themselves or others.

We joined this journey together because we see a very real, deeply ingrained problem in our culture. The well from which our sons drink is polluted and infecting them. We came together to clean the well, from the bottom up. This process takes time, flexibility, and trial and error. The thing is, we really won't know the result for years. But my hope is that with thought, a little change at home, and lots of love and connection, we have the power to make the world a better place—a healthier, more equitable environment for everyone. And you have a hand in that. So do I. Let's stay connected through that mission and know that there are many parents, dare I say most parents, who want the same. Let's be the leaders to speak up and do something. Thank you for caring. Thank you for working to change the world. Thank you for reading. Feminist boys are our future men.

Acknowledgments

To my most important mentors—Cam, Ty, and Eve—thank you for sharing your life with me and the rest of the world. You all are blooming agents of change and make the world a better place just by being you. I am so proud to be your mum. I love you more than anything.

To Mark—thank you for bearing with me as I would disappear for days on end to write. Covering the kids, learning alongside me about feminism and parenting, and engaging me in heated debates. These are the conversations that fuel thought and challenge me in frustrating and important ways. Thank you for all that you do to support me, in this book, and in the shared journey we call life. Love you tons.

Thank you Jennye Garibaldi for reaching out and engaging me on this project! I am honored, excited, and so appreciative for all your continued guidance. And a huge thanks to all the people at New Harbinger (Jennifer Holder, Marisa Solís, and the team) who were always responsive and provided much needed guardrails as I found my way through my first book.

And Sally Ekus—thank you for taking a chance on me! Being accepted by such a smart, aware, kind literary agent who really helped shape my writing journey was a stroke of luck.

And to all the amazing contributors who helped research, edit, and write alongside me. Charlotte Bingaman—what a workhorse you are. Your ability to take huge, amorphous concepts and titrate them down into actionable items is uncanny. Thank you for all your help. And Alex Coakley, Anne Drescher, Galya Atanasova, and Annie Medina—I so appreciate your wisdom and willingness to share it with me.

My friends and family who are always beside me—thank you. Thank you for so many honest conversations that help me grow as a person, psychologist, parent, friend, and advocate.

And to all the parents in this together with me—thank you. My patients, my friends, the people who read my articles—we are in this together, finding our way, trying to build a better community for us all. Thank you for reading, caring, and joining the ride with me. XO.

Glossary[145]

Ally: A person who may not share the sexual orientation, gender identity, or ethnocultural background of minorities (LGBTQI+, racial minorities, any marginalized group) but who supports and honors diversity and challenges phobic remarks and behaviors.

Bisexual: A person who has significant sexual, romantic, and/or spiritual attractions to both men and women, or someone who identifies as a member of this community.

Cisgender: A person whose gender identity aligns with the one assigned to them at birth.

Coming out: The process of disclosing one's sexual orientation or gender identity to other people.

Discrimination: The different and unfair treatment of certain groups of people based on specific characteristics, such as race, religion, age, sex, disability, sexual orientation, and/or gender identity.

Equal protection: A constitutional guarantee that the government will treat one person or group of people the same way that it would treat any other person or group of people under the same circumstances.

Feminism: The belief in social, economic, and political equality for all genders and sexes.

Gay: A term that can be used to describe either a man whose primary sexual and romantic attraction is to other men, or to reference anyone whose primary sexual and romantic attraction is to a person who is the same sex as themselves.

Gender: A set of social, physical, psychological, and emotional traits, often influenced by societal expectations, that classify an individual as feminine, masculine, androgynous, or other.

Gender dysphoria: Clinically significant distress that is caused by a person's assigned gender at birth not matching the one with which they identify.

Gender expansive: Gender identity or expression that is wider than that of the binary gender system (male/female) and is sometimes used instead of gender nonbinary.

Gender expression: The outward manifestation of internal gender identity through clothing, hairstyle, mannerisms, and other characteristics.

Gender-fluid: Term used by people who identify their gender as fluid within a spectrum of gender identities and expression. Gender-fluid people may or may not also identify as transgender.

Gender identity: An individual's inner sense of being male, female, or another gender. Gender identity is not necessarily the same as the sex assigned or presumed at birth. Everyone has a gender identity.

Gender-nonconforming: Behaving in a way that does not match social stereotypes about female or male gender, usually through dress or physical appearance.

Gender role: The social expectation of how an individual should look or behave, often based upon the sex assigned at birth.

Gender confirmation/transition: Describes both a shift over time from occupying the social role of one gender to that of another and to the medical procedures that sometimes accompany that shift. Transition may or may not include medical or legal aspects such as taking hormones, having surgeries, or changing identity documents to reflect one's gender identity.

Heterosexism: The assumption that sexuality between people of different sexes is normal, standard, superior, or universal, and that other sexual orientations are substandard, inferior, abnormal, marginal, or invalid.

Homophobia: A fear of or hostility toward lesbian, gay, and/or bisexual people, often expressed as discrimination, harassment, and violence.

Intersex: An umbrella term used to describe a wide range of natural bodily variations. Intersex people are born with sex characteristics that do not fit typical binary notions of bodies designated "male" or "female." In some cases, intersex traits are visible at birth, while in others they are not apparent until puberty. Some intersex variations may not be visibly apparent at all. Some people who are intersex identify as binary; others do not. People with intersex conditions should not be assumed to be transgender.

Lesbian: A woman whose primary sexual and romantic attraction is to other women.

LGBTQI+: The abbreviation of the lesbian, gay, bisexual, trans, queer/questioning, and intersex community.

Nonbinary: People who identify with a gender outside of the gender binary (male/female).

Out: A description for someone who expresses, or does not hide, his or her sexual orientation or gender identity.

Pansexual: A person who has the potential for emotional, romantic, or sexual attraction to people of any gender, though not necessarily simultaneously, in the same way, or to the same degree.

Pride: The idea, and events celebrating the idea, that people should be proud of their sexual orientation and/or gender identity.

Queer: A traditionally pejorative term for LGBTQI+ people that has been reclaimed by some LGBTQI+ activists who use it self-descriptively as a means to empower the LGBTQI+ community.

Questioning: A term that describes someone who is unsure of his or her sexual orientation or gender identity.

Title IX: A federal law that prohibits sex discrimination in any educational program or activity that receives assistance from the federal government.

Transgender: Refers to people whose gender identity differs from their assigned or presumed sex at birth.

Transgender man: Describes the trajectory of a person who is changing or has changed their body and lived gender role from a birth-assigned female to an affirmed male. Also, trans male, trans man, FTM, or transman.

Transgender woman: Describes the trajectory of a person who is changing or has changed their body and lived gender role from a birth-assigned male to an affirmed female. Also, trans woman, MTF, or trans female.

Transphobia: The fear or hatred of transgender people, often expressed as discrimination, harassment, and violence.

Sex: The label—male or female—a person is assigned at birth by a doctor based on their genitalia and chromosomal makeup.

Sexual orientation: An inherent, enduring emotional, romantic, or sexual attraction to other people.

Sex Talk with Kids Cheat Sheet

Talking with your son about sex and sexuality using a feminist framework is really important. You might be stumped, though, when caught off guard. Tell your child, "I'm so glad you asked about that. I want to explain that to you—can we talk about that a little later today?" Then you can turn to this cheat sheet, organized by sexual development milestones and common behaviors by age, to find effective ways to respond.

Sexual Behavior	
0 to 4 Years Old	**What Parents Can Say**
"Potty talk": talking about genitals, pee, poop	Try not to laugh. In a neutral tone ask, "Do you have questions about your penis? You seem to be really interested in talking about it. A lot of little boys your age have questions. It is super normal. But there is a time and place for all conversations. It is okay to ask me, or Daddy, or Dr. _____ about your penis, but otherwise it's usually private talk."
Touching genitals with hands and objects, "humping"	Manage your own internal freak-out and nonchalantly say, "I know it feels nice to rub your penis, honey. And that is something we do in private—in the bathroom or your bedroom."
Being curious about their own genitals and others, asking questions	"I am so glad you are asking questions. You are at the exact age when boys get curious about their penis, how it works, and how other people are built." "Everybody's body is different, but girls usually have vaginas and boys have penises."
Wanting to touch others	"I know you are so curious about other people's bodies now. And that is okay. You just have to ask first. And we don't touch other people's private parts."
Lack of awareness of touching self	"I know it feels good to touch your penis. Many boys feel that way. That is something you do in private though." For infants, teach the appropriate names for genitals: "That is your penis."

4 to 6 Years Old	What Parents Can Say
Touching self publicly or privately	If done in public: "I know it feels good to touch your penis, but that is something people do in private."
	If done in private (for example, at bedtime when you are there), resist the urge to say anything. This will eventually self-remedy. It is the cost-benefit of sitting with your discomfort versus potentially shaming your son.
Trying to see people naked	"I see you watching me. My body is different than yours is. I am a woman and have breasts and a vagina. You are a boy and have a penis. Interesting, huh? Do you have any questions?"
Mimicking kissing, hugging, and so forth	"You have so much love to give and that is great! And we have to make sure your friend wants to be kissed. Did you ask?"
	And/or depending on the situation: "We don't usually kiss friends like that—some people kiss like that when they're older and dating."
	And/or: "There are different rules at different places. Kissing friends at school is not allowed. We have to keep our bodies to ourselves there."
"Playing doctor": touching other kids' private parts in play	Stay calm and say, "Okay, it is time to get dressed. It is normal to be curious about each other's private parts, but we don't touch them. I have a book that we can learn from together."

6 to 12 Years Old	What Parents Can Say
Masturbation, privately	"It feels good to touch your penis. That is how penises are built. We do that in private. And also, make sure to wash your hands afterward."
Sexualized games	To younger kids: "I know you are so curious about bodies right now—many boys are at this age. It's not allowed to look at or touch our friend's genitals because it can make them feel uncomfortable."
Trying to see people naked	"I know you are interested in understanding about bodies right now. That is great, and we have to respect people's privacy. Let's look at your book together and talk."
	It is okay to change in front of your child in a casual, nonsexual way. That is quite different than your child seeing his friends naked and touching. In some ways, it normalizes bodies and shows we are all built differently. Of course, we would never show our body in any way that could be perceived as sexualized. Follow your child's lead here—their comfort/discomfort. Once boys hit puberty, they are most likely going to be uncomfortable with this and want more boundaries and privacy between himself and parents. It is a great message to him that he can assert his boundaries and keep himself safe.
Looking at naked pictures or sending naked pictures	Talk about the importance of never sending naked pictures. Ask your child to let you know if he receives any naked pictures.
	"Sometimes kids think it is funny to send or receive naked pictures. The thing is, that is actually against the law and can get you in big trouble. Plus, you never know who will see those pictures. Once you put them out there, you have no control of them anymore. Imagine if someone sent one to your teacher or someone in class? Yikes!"

Looking and listening to sexualized content on TV, in games, online, and via other media	To younger kids: "Computers and iPads are great in so many ways, but they can also expose us to things we don't want to see and might even scare us. At some point, you will come across adult things—naked people, maybe even people having sex. If that happens, don't worry—just close the window and you can tell me."
	Ten-year-olds and older: "You might see things online that you are curious about—people having sex. Some of it might seem scary and sometimes it might be interesting to watch and even make you want to touch your penis. The thing is—those videos are for adults who have more experience with sex, and it can be confusing to kids and even send the wrong message. Oftentimes women seem like they are being punished or even hurt. It's important to know that sex can be really fun and pleasurable. And my hope is that that is the kind of sex you have one day when you are older."
First crush: interest or attraction to peers	"It is exciting to feel feelings for somebody, isn't it? I am happy for you. What do you like about the person?"
Wanting privacy while changing	"Many kids want privacy while they change as they get older and that is completely okay. I'll give it to you."
Embarrassment and avoidance of talking about sex	"I know sex can be kind of embarrassing to talk about. I felt that way when I was a kid too, but it doesn't have to be. It is something we all go through. I am here for you to talk to whenever you are ready."

12 to 18 Years Old	What Parents Can Say
Masturbation, private	It is a normal behavior. Done privately. Give the boy privacy and move on. If you accidentally walk into his room while he is masturbating, just say "sorry" and close the door. Knock next time. No need to discuss.
Pornography, private but sometimes with friends	Talk with him about the kinds of porn, how people are viewed in them, and how it affects how he feels about and sees himself and others. "It is so normal for boys to be curious about sex. Watching pornography can both feel good and help you learn about sexuality. Do you ever watch porn? What have you seen? How do you feel while you are watching it and after? Do you think what you have seen is representative of real-life sex and relationships? Much of what we see in porn is like watching any other type of movie—it is fiction, staged, and made to portray a specific experience. Real-life sex is often different. What do you think?"
Sexual experiences	"Is anyone dating or hooking up with anyone these days? Are you interested in anyone?" Be direct and nonjudgmental: "Have you hooked up with anyone before? Have you had sex with anyone yet? What was it like? What do you hope for? Do you know how to keep yourself safe? What do you know about STDs, pregnancy, emotional safety, relational safety? Can we think about this together? How can I support you in this?"
Gender-based issues	"How do you think about gender? What do you know and how do you know that? How do you define your gender? Do you know people who have different genders than you? Who? Has anyone ever teased you about your gender? Have you ever teased anyone about their gender? If so, how do you think that affected them? Imagine if someone did that to you, what would it feel like?"

Language around boundaries, consent, and saying no	"How do you think about consent and boundaries? How do you know if you are hooking up with someone who wants to be hooking up? What if you don't want to hook up with someone? How do you say no? What are your options?"
Healthy versus unhealthy relationships	"How do you define a healthy relationship? What is important to you? What could you do to get the type of relationship you want? What can you control and what can't you control? Is there any relationship you admire? If so, why? What is love and what is intense attraction? What does it mean to be an ethical person in a relationship? What does an unhealthy relationship look like? What makes it unhealthy? How do you know when you no longer want to be with someone? How could you communicate that?"
Sexual harassment and assault	"Has anyone ever sexually harassed or assaulted you? How do you think about harassment and assault? How would you know if you were harassed or if you assaulted someone?"
Alcohol and sex	"I am curious if people in your friend group drink or use drugs. If so, which ones? How do you think about this? Have you ever drank or used drugs? Are you interested in them? What makes you curious? Is there anything you are fearful about? How do you think drinking and using drugs affects how you treat other people? How other people treat you?"
Empathy for others	"Have you ever wondered what it would be like to live in someone else's shoes for the day? Someone completely different than you? Really imagine it for a minute. What do you think it feels like being a girl? How would your day be easier? More difficult? What do you think they deal with that you don't? Is there something you wish boys would do to make your life better or easier? If so, what?"

Love	"Have you ever loved someone? What does it feel like? What do you imagine it feeling like? How would you know? What would be the upside and downside of it?"
Respect	"Do you see yourself as a respectful person? What does a respectful person look like? Who do you think is really respectful and what do they do? How important is being respectful to you? Why is it important and how can you show someone respect? How can you be respectful of people of different genders?"
Morality	"We all have an internal belief system—what we think is right and wrong. What are your most important values? Why? How did you pick them? What do you think your parents' values are? Why? How important is it for you to be a moral person? How can you keep yourself accountable to these values? Why is that important? How can I support you in that?"
Identity development	"There are so many different parts of an identity: gender, race, family, age, socioeconomic status, and sexuality, to name a few. What are the most important parts of your identity to you? Why? How can we support you in your identity? Do you have any identities you feel like you have to hide or keep more private? Can you tell me a little bit about them? If not, can you say what makes it hard to share? Is there anything I can do to make it easier to share or talk about? Has anyone ever teased or hurt you for being who you are?"

Endnotes

1   Joshua A. Krisch, "Are Most Men Sexist? Not If You Ask Them (but Yes)," Fatherly, December 13, 2018, https://www.fatherly.com/health-science/are-most-men-sexist-gender-equality-metoo/.

2   Venkatraman Chandra-Mouli et al., "Implications of the Global Early Adolescent Study's Formative Research Findings for Action and for Research," *Journal of Adolescent Health* 61, no. 4 (October 1, 2017): S5–9, https://doi.org/10.1016/j.jadohealth.2017.07.012.

3   Robert W. Blum, Kristin Mmari, and Caroline Moreau, "It Begins at 10: How Gender Expectations Shape Early Adolescence Around the World," *The Journal of Adolescent Health* 61, no. 4 Suppl (October 2017): S3–4, https://doi.org/10.1016/j.jadohealth.2017.07.009.

4   Blum, Mmari, and Moreau, "It Begins at 10."

5   Albert Bandura, "Observational Learning," in *The International Encyclopedia of Communication*, ed. W. Donsbach (Atlanta, GA: American Cancer Society, 2008), https://doi.org/10.1002/9781405186407.wbieco004.

6   Martie G. Haselton, Daniel Nettle, and Damian R. Murray, "The Evolution of Cognitive Bias," in *The Handbook of Evolutionary Psychology*, ed. D. M. Buss (Atlanta, GA: American Cancer Society, 2015): 1–20, https://doi.org/10.1002/9781119125563.evpsych241.

7   Brian A. Nosek et al., "Pervasiveness and Correlates of Implicit Attitudes and Stereotypes," *European Review of Social Psychology* 18, no. 1 (November 2007): 21, https://doi.org/10.1080/10463280701489053.

8   Birkan Tunç et al., "Establishing a Link Between Sex-Related Differences in the Structural Connectome and Behaviour," *Philosophical Transactions of the Royal Society B: Biological Sciences* 371, no. 1688 (February 19, 2016): 20150111, https://doi.org/10.1098/rstb.2015.0111.

9   Cheryl Staats, "Understanding Implicit Bias: What Educators Should Know," *The Education Digest* 82, no. 1 (2016): 29–38.

10   Staats, "Understanding Implicit Bias: What Educators Should Know."

11   Nosek et al., "Pervasiveness and Correlates of Implicit Attitudes and Stereotypes."

12   Daniel J. Siegel and Mary Hartzell, *Parenting from the Inside Out: How a Deeper Self-Understanding Can Help You Raise Children Who Thrive: 10th Anniversary Edition* (New York: Penguin, 2013), XVI.

13   Lehigh University, "'Good Enough' Parenting Is Good Enough, Study Finds," *ScienceDaily* May 8, 2019, https://www.sciencedaily.com/releases/2019/05/190508134511.htm.

14   Siegel and Hartzell, *Parenting from the Inside Out.*

15   Daniel J. Siegel, "Attachment and Self-Understanding: Parenting with the Brain in Mind," *Psychotherapy in Australia* 12, no. 2 (February 2006): 26.

16   Megan E. Baril, Ann C. Crouter, and Susan M. McHale, "Processes Linking Adolescent Well-Being, Marital Love, and Coparenting," *Journal of Family Psychology* 21, no. 4 (December 2007): 645–54, https://doi.org/10.1037/0893-3200.21.4.645.

17   "How Working Parents Share Parenting and Household Responsibilities," *Pew Research Center's Social & Demographic Trends Project* (blog), November 4, 2015, https://www.pewsocialtrends.org/2015/11/04/raising-kids-and-running-a-household-how-working-parents-share-the-load/.

18   David S. Pedulla and Sarah Thébaud, "Can We Finish the Revolution? Gender, Work-Family Ideals, and Institutional Constraint," *American Sociological Review* 80, no. 1 (February 1, 2015): 116–39, https://doi.org/10.1177/0003122414564008.

19   "How Working Parents Share Parenting and Household Responsibilities."

20   ibid

21   Pedulla and Thébaud, "Can We Finish the Revolution?"

22   Daniel L. Carlson et al., "The Gendered Division of Housework and Couples' Sexual Relationships: A Reexamination," *Journal of Marriage and Family* 78, no. 4 (2016): 975–95, https://doi.org/10.1111/jomf.12313.

23   George E. Vaillant, Charles C. McArthur, and Arlie Bock, "Grant Study of Adult Development, 19382000," May 7, 2019, https://doi.org/10.7910/DVN/48WRX9.

24   Shannon Andrus, Charlotte Jacobs, and Peter Kuriloff, "Miles to Go: The Continuing Quest for Gender Equity in the Classroom," *Phi Delta Kappan* 100, no. 2 (October 2018): 46–50, https://doi.org/10.1177/0031721718803570.

25   Making Caring Common, "Resources for Educators," December 2, 2019, https://mcc.gse.harvard.edu/resources-for-educators.

26   "Resources for Educators."

27   Warlene D. Gary and Robert Witherspoon, *The Power of Family School Community Partnerships: A Training Resource Manual* (Washington, D.C.: National Education Association, 2011), http://www2.nea.org/mediafiles/pdf/FSCP_Manual_2012.pdf.

28   "The Origin of the Term 'Intersectionality,'" *Columbia Journalism Review*, November 29, 2019, https://www.cjr.org/language_corner/intersectionality.php.

29   Jeannie Suk Gersen, "Shutting Down Conversations About Rape at Harvard Law," *New Yorker*, December 11, 2015, https://www.newyorker.com/news/news-desk/argument-sexual-assault-race-harvard-law-school.

30   Emily Yoffe, "The Question of Race in Campus Sexual-Assault Cases," *The Atlantic*, September 11, 2017, https://www.theatlantic.com/education/archive/2017/09/the-question-of-race-in-campus-sexual-assault-cases/539361/.

31   Susan M. Blake et al., "Effects of a Parent-Child Communications Intervention on Young Adolescents' Risk for Early Onset of Sexual Intercourse," *Family Planning Perspectives* 33, no. 2 (2001): 52–61, https://doi.org/10.2307/2673750.

32   John S. Santelli et al., "Does Sex Education Before College Protect Students from Sexual Assault in College?," *PLoS ONE* 13, no. 11 (November 14, 2018), https://doi.org/10.1371/journal.pone.0205951.

33   Planned Parenthood, "What Should I Teach My High School-Aged Teen about Pregnancy and Reproduction?" accessed July 28, 2020, https://www.plannedparenthood.org/learn/parents/high-school/what-should-i-teach-my-high-school-aged-teen-about-pregnancy-and.

34   Ellen K. Wilson et al., "Parents' Perspectives on Talking to Preteenage Children About Sex," *Perspectives on Sexual and Reproductive Health* 42, no. 1 (2010): 56–63, https://doi.org/10.1363/4205610.

35   Jean Piaget, "Part I: Cognitive Development in Children: Piaget Development and Learning," *Journal of Research in Science Teaching* 2, no. 3 (1964): 176–86, https://doi.org/10.1002/tea.3660020306.

36   ibid

37   Angel Nga-Man Leung and Henry K. S. Ng, "Sex Role Development and Education," in *International Encyclopedia of the Social & Behavioral Sciences (Second Edition)*, ed. James D. Wright (Oxford: Elsevier, 2015): 678–85, https://doi.org/10.1016/B978-0-08-097086-8.92014-2.

38   Piaget, "Part I."

39   Gertrude G. Zeinstra et al., "Cognitive Development and Children's Perceptions of Fruit and Vegetables: A Qualitative Study," *International Journal of Behavioral Nutrition and Physical Activity* 4, no. 1 (July 9, 2007): 30, https://doi.org/10.1186/1479-5868-4-30.

40   René van der Veer and Jaan Valsiner, *Understanding Vygotsky: A Quest for Synthesis*, (Malden: Blackwell Publishing, 1991).

41   APA Dictionary of Psychology, "Psychosocial Development," November 29, 2019, https://dictionary.apa.org/psychosocial-development.

42   Suzanne E. Vogel-Scibilia et al., "The Recovery Process Utilizing Erikson's Stages of Human Development," *Community Mental Health Journal* 45, no. 6 (June 17, 2009): 405, https://doi.org/10.1007/s10597-009-9189-4.

43   Ronald F. Duska and Mariellen Whelan, *Moral Development: A Guide to Piaget and Kohlberg* (New York: Paulist, 1975).

44   Emily Nagoski, a prominent sex researcher and educator, says we are shaped by the moral, medical, and media messages we receive as kids. Her book, *Come as You Are: The Surprising New Science That Will Transform Your Sex Life* is worth a read for every woman (and anyone who wants to please one). Although she writes mainly to women, she has a chapter called "Cultural Context: A Sex-Positive Life in a Sex-Negative World" that relates to all sexualities.

45   National Child Traumatic Stress Network, *Sexual Development and Behavior in Children: Information for Parents and Caregivers*, 2009, https://www.nctsn.org/resources/sexual-development-and-behavior-children-information-parents-and-caregivers.

46   "Sexual Development and Behavior in Children."

47   J. E. R. Staddon and D. T. Cerutti, "Operant Conditioning," *Annual Review of Psychology* 54, no. 1 (2003): 115–44, https://doi.org/10.1146/annurev.psych.54.101601.145124.

48   Robert Weiss, "The Prevalence of Porn," *Psych Central*, March 28, 2019, https://blogs.psychcentral.com/sex/2013/05/the-prevalence-of-porn/.

49   Michael Lucas, "On Gay Porn," *Yale Journal of Law and Feminism* 18 (2006): 299.

50   "The Most Up-to-Date Pornography Statistics," *Covenant Eyes*, November 29, 2019, https://www.covenanteyes.com/pornstats/.

51   Lucas, "On Gay Porn."

52   ibid

53   It was at Esther Perel's Sessions Live Conference in New York, 2019.

54   Lucas, "On Gay Porn."

55   Larry Greenemeier, "Remembering the Day the World Wide Web Was Born," *Scientific American*, November 29, 2019, https://www.scientificamerican.com/article/day-the-web-was-born/.

56   Making Caring Common, "The Talk: How Adults Can Promote Young People's Healthy Relationships and Prevent Misogyny and Sexual Harassment," November 27, 2019, https://mcc.gse.harvard.edu/reports/the-talk.

57   Nancy J. Evans and Vernon A. Wall, eds., *Beyond Tolerance: Gays, Lesbians, and Bisexuals on Campus* (Alexandria, VA: American College Personnel Association, 1991).

58   Joanne L. Bagshaw, *The Feminist Handbook: Practical Tools to Resist Sexism and Dismantle the Patriarchy* (Oakland, CA: New Harbinger Publications, 2019).

59   Michele C. Black et al., *The National Intimate Partner and Sexual Violence Survey (NISVS): 2010 Summary Report* (Atlanta, GA: National Center for Injury Prevention and Control, U.S. Centers for Disease Control and Prevention, 2010).

60   K. Nicole Jones, Melanie E. Brewster, and Jacob A. Jones, "The Creation and Validation of the LGBT Ally Identity Measure," *Psychology of Sexual Orientation and Gender Diversity* 1, no. 2 (June 2014): 181–95, https://doi.org/10.1037/sgd0000033.

61   Momentous Institute, "What Is Attunement?," February 27, 2017, accessed March 1, 2020, https://momentousinstitute.org/blog/what-is-attunement.

62   Mary D. Salter Ainsworth, "Infant-Mother Attachment," *American Psychologist* 34 (1979), https://pdfs.semanticscholar.org/5576/ca056c7c286e0e73dd0b1a4236f324d32280.pdf.

63   Walter F. Mondale, "S.626 - 94th Congress (1975-1976): Child and Family Services Act," February 7, 1975, https://www.congress.gov/bill/94th-congress/senate-bill/626.

64   Mary D. Salter Ainsworth, "Infant-Mother Attachment."

65   "Second Generation Study," Harvard Second Generation Study, 2015, https://www.adultdevelopmentstudy.org.

66   "Relationship of Emotional Intelligence with Self-Esteem Among Adolescents," ResearchGate, February 24, 2020, https://www.researchgate.net/publication/309242131_Relationship_of_emotional_intelligence_with_self_esteem_among_adolescents.

67   John Gottman, *Raising an Emotionally Intelligent Child* (New York: Simon and Schuster, 2011).

68   Tamra J. Sillick and Nicola S. Schutte, "Emotional Intelligence and Self-Esteem Mediate Between Perceived Early Parental Love and Adult Happiness," *E-Journal of Applied Psychology* 2, no. 2 (2006): 38–48, https://hdl.handle.net/1959.11/2950.

69   APA *Dictionary of Psychology*, s.v. "self-awareness," accessed February 24, 2020, https://dictionary.apa.org/self-awareness.

70   APA *Dictionary of Psychology*, s.v. "self-regulation," accessed February 24, 2020, https://dictionary.apa.org/self-regulation.

71   APA *Dictionary of Psychology*, s.v. "motivation," accessed February 24, 2020, https://dictionary.apa.org/motivation.

72   APA *Dictionary of Psychology*, s.v. "empathy," accessed February 24, 2020, https://dictionary.apa.org/empathy.

73   APA *Dictionary of Psychology*, s.v. "social skills," accessed February 24, 2020, https://dictionary.apa.org/social-skills.

74   Moshe Zeidner et al., "Development of Emotional Intelligence: Towards a Multi-Level Investment Model," *Human Development* 46, no. 2–3 (2003): 69–96, https://doi.org/10.1159/000068580.

75   Mick Cooper et al., *The Handbook of Person-Centred Psychotherapy and Counselling* (Victoria, Australia: Macmillan International Higher Education, 2013).

76   Daniela Rocha Lopes, Kees van Putten, and Peter Paul Moormann, "The Impact of Parental Styles on the Development of Psychological Complaints," *Europe's Journal of Psychology* 11, no. 1 (February 27, 2015): 155–68, https://doi.org/10.5964/ejop.v11i1.836.

77   K. Jones, M. Brewster, and J. Jones, "The Creation and Validation of the LGBT Ally Identity Measure," *Psychology of Sexual Orientation and Gender Diversity* 1, no. (2014): 181–195, https://doi.org/10.1037/sgd0000033.

78   "Gender Pay Gap Statistics for 2020," *PayScale* (blog), accessed August 2, 2020, https://www.payscale.com/data/gender-pay-gap.

79   ibid

80   U.S. Census Bureau, "Gaps in the Wealth of Americans by Household Type," accessed August 2, 2020, https://www.census.gov/library/stories/2019/08/gaps-in-wealth-americans-by-household-type.html.

81   Drew Desilver and Kristen Bialek, "Blacks, Hispanics Face Mortgage Challenges," *Pew Research Center* (blog), accessed October 4, 2020, https://www.pewresearch.org/fact-tank/2017/01/10/blacks-and-hispanics-face-extra-challenges-in-getting-home-loans/.

82   Kristin Bialik, "For the Fifth Time in a Row, the New Congress Is the Most Racially and Ethnically Diverse Ever," *Pew Research Center* (blog), February 8, 2018, https://www.pewresearch.org/fact-tank/2019/02/08/for-the-fifth-time-in-a-row-the-new-congress-is-the-most-racially-and-ethnically-diverse-ever/.

83   LaGarrett J. King, "The Status of Black History in U.S. Schools and Society," *Social Education*, n.d., 5.

84   Christopher Ingraham, "Black Men Sentenced to More Time for Committing the Exact Same Crime as a White Person, Study Finds," *Washington Post*, November 16, 2017, https://www.washingtonpost.com/news/wonk/wp/2017/11/16/black-men-sentenced-to-more-time-for-committing-the-exact-same-crime-as-a-white-person-study-finds/.

85   U.S. Centers for Disease Control and Prevention, "Communities, Schools, Workplaces, & Events," April 30, 2020, https://www.cdc.gov/coronavirus/2019-ncov/community/health-equity/race-ethnicity.html.

86   Boele De Raad, *The Big Five Personality Factors: The Psycholexical Approach to Personality* (Ashland, OH: Hogrefe & Huber Publishers, 2000).

87   "Big Five Personality Test," accessed April 5, 2020, https://openpsychometrics.org/tests/IPIP-BFFM/.

88   Maud Purcell, "The Health Benefits of Journaling," *PsychCentral*, July 29, 2020, https://psychcentral.com/lib/the-health-benefits-of-journaling.

89   American Psychological Association, APA *Guidelines for Psychological Practice with Boys and Men* (Washington, DC: American Psychological Association, Boys and Men Guidelines Group, 2018).

90   APA, APA *Guidelines for Psychological Practice with Boys and Men.*

91   Kristin D. Neff, Kristin L. Kirkpatrick, and Stephanie S. Rude, "Self-Compassion and Adaptive Psychological Functioning," *Journal of Research in Personality* 41, no. 1 (February 1, 2007): 139–54, https://doi.org/10.1016/j.jrp.2006.03.004.

92   Kristin D. Neff and Roos Vonk, "Self-Compassion Versus Global Self-Esteem: Two Different Ways of Relating to Oneself," *Journal of Personality* 77, no. 1 (2009): 23–50, https://doi.org/10.1111/j.1467-6494.2008.00537.x.

93   IFS Institute, "The Internal Family Systems Model Outline," accessed October 4, 2020 from https://ifs-institute.com/resources/articles/internal-family-systems-model-outline.

94   Esther L. Meerwijk and Jae M. Sevelius, "Transgender Population Size in the United States: A Meta-Regression of Population-Based Probability Samples," *American Journal of Public Health* 107, no. 2 (February 2017): e1–8, https://doi.org/10.2105/AJPH.2016.303578.

95   Sharon Smith et al., *National Intimate Partner and Sexual Violence Survey: 2015 Data Brief—Updated Release*" (Atlanta, GA: National Center for Injury Prevention and Control Centers for Disease Control and Prevention, 2018), https://www.cdc.gov/violenceprevention/pdf/2015data-brief508.pdf.

96   Liz Plank, "Most Perpetrators of Sexual Violence Are Men, so Why Do We Call It a Women's Issue? - Divided States of Women," *Divided States of Women*, November 2, 2017, https://www.dividedstatesofwomen.com/2017/11/2/16597768/sexual-assault-men-himthough.

97   Richard Weissbourd , and Alison Cashin, "5 Ways Parents Can Help Kids Understand Consent and Prevent Sexual Assault," *The Washington Post*, October 16, 2018, https://www.washingtonpost.com/lifestyle/2018/10/16/ways-parents-can-help-kids-understand-consent-prevent-sexual-assault/.

98   Peggy Orenstein, "The Miseducation of the American Boy," *The Atlantic*, December 20, 2019, https://www.theatlantic.com/magazine/archive/2020/01/the-miseducation-of-the-american-boy/603046/.

99   Kim Parker, Juliana Horowitz, and Renee Stepler, "Americans See Different Expectations for Men and Women," Pew Research Center, December 5, 2017, https://www.pewsocialtrends.org/2017/12/05/americans-see-different-expectations-for-men-and-women/.

100   Perry Undem, "The State of Gender Equality for U.S. Adolescents," Plan International, September 12, 2018, https://www.planusa.org/docs/state-of-gender-equality-2018.pdf.

101   Perry Undem, "The State of Gender Equality for U.S. Adolescents."

102   Peggy Orenstein, "The Miseducation of the American Boy."

103   Dakin Andone, "Girls Can Join the Boy Scouts Now - But Not Everyone Is Happy about It," *Cable News Network*, February 1, 2019, https://www.cnn.com/2019/02/01/us/boy-scouts-girls-trnd/index.html.

104   Perry Undem, "The State of Gender Equality for U.S. Adolescents," 6.

105   Sarah Rich, "Today's Masculinity Is Stifling," *The Atlantic*, June 11, 2018, https://www.theatlantic.com/family/archive/2018/06/imagining-a-better-boyhood/562232/.

106   Sarah Rich, "Today's Masculinity Is Stifling."

107   WGB Staff, "Does Food Have a Gender?" Winsight Grocery Business, March 3, 2020, https://www.winsightgrocerybusiness.com/products/does-food-have-gender.

108   ibid

109   ibid

110   ibid

111   ibid

112   ibid

113   ibid

114   Peggy Orenstein, "The Miseducation of the American Boy."

115   ibid

116   Katie Hoeppner, "Standing Up to the Man: How Three Female Attorneys Fought Back Against Rampant Sexism at a New Mexico District Attorney's Office." ACLU, May 30, 2019, https://www.aclu-nm.org/en/news/standing-man-how-three-female-attorneys-fought-back-against-rampant-sexism-new-mexico-district.

117   Peggy Orenstein, "It's Not That Men Don't Know What Consent Is," *The New York Times*, February 23, 2019. https://www.nytimes.com/2019/02/23/opinion/sunday/sexual-consent-college.html.

118   ibid

119   Richard Weissbourd, Trisha Ross Anderson, Alison Cahsin, and Joe McIntyre. "The Talk: How Adults Can Promote Young People's Healthy Relationships and Prevent Misogyny and Sexual Harassment," Making Caring Common Project, n.d., 3, https://static1.squarespace.com/static/5b7c56e255b02c683659fe43/t/5bd51a0324a69425bd079b59/1540692500558/mcc_the_talk_final.pdf.

120   Richard Weissbourd and Alison Cashin, "5 Ways Parents Can Help Kids Understand Consent and Prevent Sexual Assault."

121   Planned Parenthood, "Sexual Consent," n.d. https://www.plannedparenthood.org/learn/relationships/sexual-consent. Used with permission.

122   Paul Bergman, "Assault, Battery, and Aggravated Assault," NOLO blog, n.d. https://www.nolo.com/legal-encyclopedia/assault-battery-aggravated-assault-33775.html.

123   Richard Weissbourd et al., "The Talk: How Adults Can Promote Young People's Healthy Relationships and Prevent Misogyny and Sexual Harassment."

124   Robert Weiss, "The Prevalence of Porn," *Psych Central*, March 28, 2019, https://blogs.psychcentral.com/sex/2013/05/the-prevalence-of-porn/.

125   Ann Swidler, "Culture in Action: Symbols and Strategies," *American Sociological Review* (1986): 273–286.

126   Common Sense Media. "The Common Sense Census: Media Use by Tweens and Teens," October 28, 2019, 3. https://www.commonsensemedia.org/sites/default/files/ uploads/research/2019-census-8-to-18-full-report-updated.pdf.

127   Common Sense Media, "The Common Sense Census: Media Use by Tweens and Teens."

128   ibid

129   Peggy Orenstein, *Boys & Sex: Young Men on Hookups, Love, Porn, Consent, and Navigating the New Masculinity,* (New York: Harper, an Imprint of HarperCollins Publishers, 2020).

130   L. Takeuchi, and Reed Stevens, *The New Coviewing: Designing For Learning Through Joint Media Engagement* (New York: The Joan Ganz Cooney Center at Sesame Workshop, 2011), https://www.joanganzcooneycenter.org/wp-content/uploads/2011/12/jgc_coviewing_desktop.pdf.

131   P. M. Valkenburg, M. Krcmar, A. L. Peeters, and N. M. Marseille, "Developing a Scale to Assess Three Styles of Television Mediation: 'Instructive Mediation,' 'Restrictive Mediation,' and 'Social Coviewing,'" *Journal of Broadcasting & Electronic Media* 43, no. 1 (1999): 52–66.

132   Takeuchi, "The New Coviewing."

133   Melissa Morgenlander,"Adult-Child Co-Viewing of Educational Television: Enhancing Preschoolers' Understanding of Mathematics Shown on *Sesame Street,*" *ProQuest LLC* (2010): 1–147.

134   Takeuchi, "The New Coviewing," 12.

135   Sonia Livingstoneand Ellen J. Helsper, "Parental Mediation of Children's Internet Use," *Journal of Broadcasting & Electronic Media* 52, no. 4 (2008): 581–599.

136   Takeuchi, "The New Coviewing," 11.

137   Education Is Our Best Friend. "Who's Piloting the Plane?" November 4, 2014. https://educationisthebestfriend.wordpress.com/2014/11/04/whos-piloting-the-plane/.

138   Lane Beckes, James A. Coan, and Karen Hasselmo, "Familiarity Promotes the Blurring of Self and Other in the Neural Representation of Threat," *Social Cognitive and Affective Neuroscience* 8, no. 6 (2013): 670–677, https://doi.org/10.1093/scan/nss046.

139   Jamil Zaki, "Making Empathy Central to Your Company Culture," *Harvard Business Review,* May 30, 2019, https://hbr.org/2019/05/making-empathy-central-to-your-company-culture.

140   Michele Borba, *Unselfie: Why Empathetic Kids Succeed in Our All-About-Me World* (New York: Touchstone, 2016).

141   Making Caring Common, "For Families: 5 Tips for Cultivating Empathy," accessed June 13, 2020, https://mcc.gse.harvard.edu/resources-for-families/5-tips-cultivating-empathy.

142   Sara H. Konrath, Edward H. O'Brien, and Courtney Hsing, "Changes in Dispositional Empathy in American College Students Over Time: A Meta-Analysis," *Personality and Social Psychology Review* 15, no. 2 (2011): 180–198, https://doi.org/10.1177/1088868310377395.

143   Jessica Joelle Alexander, *The Danish Way of Parenting: What the Happiest People in the World Know about Raising Confident, Capable Kids* (East Rutherford: Penguin Publishing Group, 2016).

144   Jennifer S. Mascaro et al., "Child Gender Influences Paternal Behavior, Language, and Brain Function," *Behavioral Neuroscience* 131, no. 3 (June 2017): 262–73, https://doi.org/10.1037/bne0000199.

145   Human Rights Campaign, "Sexual Orientation and Gender Identity Definitions," accessed April 3, 2020, https://www.hrc.org/resources/sexual-orientation-and-gender-identity-terminology-and-definitions/.

Bobbi Wegner, PsyD, is a lecturer at Harvard Graduate School of Education, supervising clinical psychologist at Boston Behavioral Medicine, writer, speaker, and cofounder of a virtual platform that provides real support for real parents from real experts. She has given three TEDx Talks on raising boys in modern culture, frequently writes on the topic, and gets much of her research from raising three children of her own (two of which are boys).

Foreword writer **Jessica Joelle Alexander** is coauthor of *The Danish Way of Parenting.*

Real change *is* possible

For more than forty-five years, New Harbinger has
published proven-effective self-help books and pioneering
workbooks to help readers of all ages and backgrounds
improve mental health and well-being, and achieve lasting
personal growth. In addition, our spirituality books
offer profound guidance for deepening awareness and
cultivating healing, self-discovery, and fulfillment.

Founded by psychologist Matthew McKay and Patrick
Fanning, New Harbinger is proud to be an independent,
employee-owned company. Our books reflect our
core values of integrity, innovation, commitment,
sustainability, compassion, and trust. Written by leaders
in the field and recommended by therapists worldwide,
New Harbinger books are practical, accessible, and
provide real tools for real change.

newharbingerpublications

MORE BOOKS from
NEW HARBINGER PUBLICATIONS

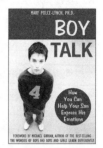

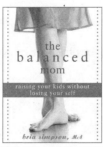

Register your **new harbinger** titles for additional benefits!

When you register your **new harbinger** title—purchased in any format, from any source—you get access to benefits like the following:

- Downloadable accessories like printable worksheets and extra content

- Instructional videos and audio files

- Information about updates, corrections, and new editions

Not every title has accessories, but we're adding new material all the time.

Access free accessories in 3 easy steps:

1. Sign in at NewHarbinger.com (or **register** to create an account).

2. Click on **register a book**. Search for your title and click the **register** button when it appears.

3. Click on the **book cover or title** to go to its details page. Click on **accessories** to view and access files.

That's all there is to it!

If you need help, visit:

NewHarbinger.com/accessories

new harbinger
CELEBRATING
40 YEARS